ENCOUNTERING

Jesus

A Life-Changing Look at the Son of God

Cheryl Price, Ph.D.
Evangeline Carey
Rosa Sailes, Ed.D.

UMI Urban Ministries, Inc.
Chicago, Illinois

Publisher
UMI (Urban Ministries, Inc.)
P. O. Box 436987
Chicago, Illinois 60643-6987
1-800-860-8642
www.urbanministries.com

First Edition
First Printing

Scriptures are from the King James Version

Encountering Jesus: A Life-Changing Look at the Son of God is a compilation and revision of the following UMI publications:
Jesus, King of Kings Leader's Guide —Based on the Gospel of Matthew
Jesus, God's Model Servant Leader's Guide —Based on the Gospel of Mark
Life in Jesus, God's Chosen Son Leader's Guide —Based on the Gospel of John
In the Beginning Leader's Guide —Based on the book of Genesis

Encountering Jesus: A Life-Changing Look at the Son of God Leader's Guide has been compiled, revised and edited by Cheryl Price, Ph.D., Evangeline Carey, and Rosa Sailes, Ed.D.

Library of Congress Cataloging-in-Publication Data

Encountering Jesus: A Life-Changing Look at the Son of God/ Cheryl Price, Ph.D., Evangeline Carey, and Rosa Sailes, Ed.D.
Includes bibliographical references.
ISBN-13: 978-1-60352-354-7
ISBN-10: 1-60352-354-5
1. Christian living 2. African American

Library of Congress Control Number: 2008949486

Printed in the United States of America.

Dedication

We dedicate this book to all the teachers of God's Holy Word with special thanks to our families who have afforded us the time and encouragement to write for Christ, to our UMI family who has also labored in this effort, and to the myriad of scholars and theologians who have helped to unfold the Scriptures.

Table of Contents

Introduction

Encountering Jesus: A Life-Changing Look at the Son of God provides an opportunity for you to discover or rediscover the miracles of Jesus as they were first experienced by those who came into direct contact with the living Savior's power and compassion. The Gospel writers you will study in this book—Matthew, Mark, and John—provide the documented accounts of these moving ministry events which impacted people then and continue to touch lives today.

Jesus calmed the raging seas that erupted on the waters and within the hearts of people. He brought life from death to those who had physically died as well as to those whose faith kept them from breathing life into their situations. Where people were filled with trembling and doubt, the power of God through Jesus brought renewed mercy and hope. The Gospel writers give us insight into Jesus' life. *Encountering Jesus: A Life-Changing Look at the Son of God* shows how Jesus continues to be the Messiah, the Savior, today through our life-changing experiences with Him!

Revisit the account of Jesus and the ancient biblical people. Travel through time to view even nature responding to the deity of Christ. As you take this journey, allow your senses to move into the depth of the encounters. Behold the power, majesty, and excitement of Jesus as you imagine yourself walking on the dusty, hot sands of Jerusalem or sailing on the rough and dangerous waters of an unexpected storm on the Sea of Galilee. Reflect on the events and their locations as you examine the lives of the people, witness Jesus' interactions, and see the Son of Man as experienced by the people of God. As you share in the adventure of Jesus' ministry, you will be compelled to share the testimony of the awesome life-changing encounter you will have with Jesus.

The Origin of the Universe

BASED ON GENESIS 1:1–15
KEY VERSE: *"In the beginning God created the heaven and the earth"* *(Genesis 1:1, KJV).*

OPENING PRAYER
Dear God, help me to know and appreciate Your hand in Creation. Thank You for giving humanity stewardship over Your masterpiece. Help us to be good stewards as you help us to preserve and protect the environment that you have provided for us. Amen.

WORDS TO CONSIDER
1. CREATION (GENESIS 1:1–2:3). Creation is all that God fashioned, formed, and produced from nothing. By an act of God, the universe came into existence. God, then, is the Originator or Creator of the universe. The Bible's chief account of Creation is found in Genesis 1:1–2:3.
2. HEAVEN (v. 1). In biblical Hebrew, the word for "heaven" is always plural. It is *shamayim* or *shameh* and means "sky—as abode of the stars, the visible universe, the atmosphere, etc." It also means "the abode of God" (Strong 1996).

INTRODUCTION
Lois attends a university in the Pacific Northwest. She has always believed that God is the Creator of the universe. However, Lois's anthropology teacher insists that the universe evolved from a cataclysmic explosion and that, through a series of erratic stages, human beings have evolved or developed into their present form without any help from God.

Lois argued vehemently for her Christian view, but it was to no avail. In fact, Lois's teacher threatened to fail her if she didn't stop talking about her Christian beliefs in the class or in her papers. Still, Lois knows what she believes and has no intention of changing her views.

For centuries, people questioned and debated the origin of the universe. But for most Christians, God's creation of the universe is not an issue for debate. Many Christians believe that evolutionists who assert that the universe just happened without God are wrong. The book of Genesis contradicts this argument. In fact, it asserts that Almighty God, the Supreme Being of all, put all the pieces of our universe together in an intricate and marvelous fashion.

By faith, Christians accept the biblical account of Creation as a fact. The Bible—God's inerrant Word—says that God created the universe and everything within it (Genesis 1:1). Because we believe that the Bible is the inspired Word of God, we—as Christians—accept the Bible's account of Creation as true.

The question of whether science contradicts the Bible is one people keep asking. The question divides both Christians and non-Christians alike. The issue is whether we can trust biblical statements when they appear to contradict what scientists regard as fact. Christians believe that God is the source of everything. That includes the physical universe and all it contains. Christians also believe that God inspired the Bible—which means, as the Apostle Paul wrote, that God breathed out the Scriptures. Since God breathed out His Word, the logical conclusion is that the original documents were accurate. What then do we do when the findings of science appear to contradict truth revealed in the Bible? Legend has it that a reporter once asked this question of a Biology professor. The response simply was that the Bible, which cannot be contradictory, is true; therefore, we must assume that either we don't have all of the facts of science or we don't fully understand the Bible.

Chapter 1 focuses on the biblical account of Creation in the book of Genesis. From the Creation story, we learn about God and how humankind fits into His overall plan.

SCRIPTURE TEXT

GENESIS 1:1, KJV In the beginning God created the heaven and the earth. **2** And the earth was without form, and void; and darkness was upon the face of the deep. And the Spirit of God moved upon the face of the waters. **3** And God said, Let there be light: and there was light. **4** And God saw the light, that it was good: and God divided the light from the darkness. **5** And God called the light Day, and the darkness he called Night. And the evening and the morning were the first day. **6** And God said, Let there be a firmament in the midst of the waters, and let it divide the waters from the waters. **7** And God made the firmament, and divided the waters which were under the firmament from the waters which were above the firmament: and it was so. **8** And God called the firmament Heaven. And the evening and the morning were the second day. **9** And God said, Let the waters under the heaven be gathered together unto one place, and let the dry land appear: and it was so. **10** And God called the dry land Earth; and the gathering together of the waters called he Seas: and God saw that it was good. **11** And God said, Let the earth bring forth grass, the herb yielding seed, and the fruit tree yielding fruit after his kind, whose seed is in itself, upon the earth: and it was so. **12** And the earth brought forth grass, and herb yielding seed after his kind, and the tree yielding fruit, whose seed was in itself, after his kind: and God saw that it was good. **13** And the evening and the morning were the third day. **14** And God said, Let there be lights in the firmament of the heaven to divide the day from the night; and let them be for signs, and for seasons, and for days, and years: **15** And let them be for lights in the firmament of the heaven to give light upon the earth: and it was so.

BIBLE BACKGROUND

The first five books of the Old Testament are called the Books of the Law, the Torah, or the Pentateuch. Genesis, then, is the first book of this larger work. Many people believe that the word *genesis* is Greek and it means "origin" or "beginning." This title was given to the book by the translators of the Greek Old Testament, which is known as the Septuagint. *Bereshith,* in both the "Hebrew and Greek forms," is "the title of Genesis (and) appropriately describes its contents, since it is primarily a book of beginnings" (*The NIV Study Bible* 1995).

Genesis reveals two major concepts: the origins of human history and God's progressive self-revelation to humanity. The book is quoted more than 60 times in the New Testament. Jesus Christ quotes many passages from it (see Matthew 19:4–6; Mark 10:4–9). Genesis provides the historical account of the beginning of God's relationship with humans; it also records the beginning of many things including the world, civilization, the nations, sin, and Israel.

Genesis contains important theological themes: "The doctrine of the living, personal God; the doctrine of humans who are made in the image of God; the doctrine of the Fall; the anticipation of a Redeemer; and the covenant promises made to the nation Israel" (Ryrie 1984). Genesis is a unique book among all the literature of the Ancient Near East and is the foundation for all other books in the Bible.

EXPLORING THE MEANING
1. THE BEGINNING OF THE UNIVERSE (GENESIS 1:1–2)
According to the Bible, "God created the heaven and the earth" (Genesis 1:1). This is an emphatically stated truth that all believers accept by faith. We can learn much about the attributes of Almighty God from this

one statement. First, our God is Creator; therefore, He is *creative*. Who but God could have brought into existence something from nothing? Second, we learn two more of His attributes: God is both *eternal* (forever and ever He will be God) and *sovereign* (He is in control and never out of control of His universe). In essence, God doesn't need anything or anyone to help Him be God. He is God all by Himself. For this alone, we can praise Him!

Third, it was Almighty God who gave both form and shape to the earth that was previously dark, formless, void, and uninhabited. In fact, Genesis 1:2 tells us that it was an "empty, formless mass cloaked in darkness" (*Life Application Study Bible* 1996). The Bible tells us that God's Spirit "hovered" or moved over the waters and was actively involved in the creation of the world. The Hebrew word for "move" is *rachaph*, which means "to brood, flutter, or shake." Even though we may never know all the answers of how God actually did His creation work, in essence, by faith, we believe that the one, supreme, true God created the heaven and the earth, just as His Word says.

The question then arises, "How long did it take Almighty God to create His world?" While the Bible tells us six days, it is not clear whether they are literal 24-hour time periods or whether they represent millions of years. Some scholars have proposed that a "Gap" exists between Genesis 1:1 and Genesis 1:2. According to scholars Ken Ham and Paul Taylor, this idea was first suggested by Dr. Thomas Chalmers of Edinburgh University. Chalmers proposed the idea to refute Darwin's Theory of Evolution, which contends that "all life is related and has descended from a common ancestor: the birds and the bananas, the fishes and the flowers are all related" (Ham and Taylor 1988). Darwin's general theory presumes the development of life from non-life forms and stresses a purely naturalistic (undirected) "descent with modification." That is, "complex creatures evolve from more simplistic ancestors naturally over time" (www.darwins-theory-of-evolution.com).

The Gap Theory suggests that a time span of millions of years exists between Genesis 1:1 and Genesis 1:2. Chalmers has asserted that, in Genesis 1:1, God first created plants and animals; but then Satan rebelled against God and was cast to Earth, causing corruption. Next, God supposedly judged with a deluge called "Lucifer's Flood," which killed all the animals and laid sediments on the earth. Thus, the majority of earth's fossils and fossil fuels were deposited at the end of the gap just before the Creation Week began in Genesis 1:2 (Ham and Taylor 1988). Despite any plausibility in the Gap Theory, we do not have conclusive evidence in Scripture to support such a theory. It is clear that the most important point is not how long it took to create the world, but that God did so—and in an orderly fashion.

2. THE BEGINNING OF LIGHT (vv. 3–5)

The first element that God created was "light." How did He create it? The Bible affirms that God spoke light into existence by saying, "Let there be light: and there was light" (Genesis 1:3). This is not the same as a casual utterance. This is the spoken word of God which has inherent in it God's thoughts and intents. From God's spoken word, matter comes into existence—fully formed and fully useful. There is no indication that the light was dim and needed refinement. God spoke light into existence. Indeed, He spoke the dawning of our world.

3. THE BEGINNING OF HEAVEN (vv. 6–8)

From Genesis 1:6, we learn that the next element God created was a "firmament in the midst of the waters." The Hebrew word for "firmament" is *raqiya,* and it means "a visible arch of the sky." Apparently, God began to separate the sky and waters so that there would be a distinction between the two just as there is a distinction between day and night. Charles Ryrie suggests that "the firmament was an open expanse of the heavens, which appeared as a vast canopy or tent above the earth" (1984). God formed the sky above and oceans beneath. When you stand on a beach and look out as far as the eye can see, the view of the horizon with the sky and waters appearing to touch one another will help you begin to grasp the vastness of God's firmament.

4. THE BEGINNING OF THE EARTH (vv. 9–13)

On the third day of Creation, God began to move the waters so that the dry land could appear and the waters could be given their special place. Scientists tell us that the earth is made up mostly of water; so in essence, God moved the waters around so the dry land could be seen. God called the dry land "earth." The Hebrew word is *erets,* and it means "country, field, land, and world" (Strong 1996).

Before God populated the earth with people, He created grass, herbs, fruit trees, and all the seeds needed to bring forth vegetation and other plant life. In spite of the attempts of some evolutionists to convince us that these things "just happened," the Bible affirms that God made the vegetation on the earth and saw that "it was good" (Genesis 1:12). Christians understand that all of the plants, grass, trees, and other greenery were made by God, and Christian scholars believe that the world is too intricate to have just happened by chance.

5. THE BEGINNING OF THE SEASONS (vv. 14–15)

On the fourth day of Creation, God the Creator replaced the light source that He made with the sun and moon. Ryrie suggests that the purpose of distinguishing day and night was so humans could get their bearings, to mark off the seasons, and to give light to the earth (1984).

The sun and moon are much needed heat and light sources, and each rotates at a fixed time and for a fixed purpose. Regardless of what certain evolutionists teach, we know that God is sovereign. He has been and continues to be in control of the universe, and all He has made is good.

POINTS TO PONDER

Since we recognize God as the Creator of all that exists, we should praise His ingenuity and power. In addition, we should do our part to preserve the earth's resources and use them for the glory of God and for the benefit of His creatures.

REFLECTIONS

You have learned a great deal about the origin of the universe and God, who created it. As you consider some of the many points that have been made, also entertain the following questions:

1. What does the Bible mean when it says "in the beginning"?
2. When, where, and how do you believe the universe was created?

DECIDING MY RESPONSIBILITY
PERSONAL

God created humanity for a purpose. That purpose is so that we can have an intimate, personal relationship with Him—we can know and worship Him. In order to cultivate that intimate relationship with God, we must know and appreciate that He is Creator of heaven and earth and all humanity.

Reflect on the various distinctions between life forms: plants, trees, birds, and animals. The fact that Almighty God created them should affect our attitude toward the preservation of our forests and endangered species. Then, consider the current state of air and water pollution, and the question of what you are doing to help your environment. Consider these suggestions: (1) Spend some special time thanking God for His creation. (2) Spend time at a community park or beach and examine the natural elements around you. Can you see God's handiwork in His creation? What can you learn from the natural surroundings? Write down your observations in a prayer journal, and praise God for the beauty of the universe that He created and made humanity a steward over.

COMMUNITY

Organize a project to enhance an area within walking distance of your church. Some suggestions: (1) Clean up a vacant lot. (2) Create or improve a playground. (3) Start a recycling program. (4) Paint or sponsor the painting of a nature or religious mural on a vacant wall. (5) Plant flowers or a tree.

CLOSING PRAYER

Thank You, God, for Your mighty hand in Creation. Help me to be diligent in carrying out my responsibilities to preserve what You have given humanity. Amen.

SOURCES

Achtemeier, Paul J. *Harper's Bible Dictionary.* New York: Harper & Row Publishers, 1985. pp. 192–193.

Ham, Ken and Taylor, Paul. *The Genesis Solution.* San Diego: Master Books, 1988. pp. 60–63.

Life Application Study Bible (New Living Translation). Wheaton, IL: Tyndale House Publishers, Inc., 1996. p. 5.

Ryrie, Charles. *Ryrie Study Bible.* Chicago: Moody Press, 1984. pp. 5, 7, 8.

"Darwin's Theory of Evolution—A Theory in Crisis." http://www.darwins-theory-of-evolution.com/ (accessed August 23, 2008).

Strong, James. *Strong's Exhaustive Concordance of the Bible.* Libronix Digital Library System. Logos Bible Software. Woodside Bible Fellowship, 1996.

The NIV Study Bible. Barker, Kenneth. Grand Rapids, MI: Zondervan Publishing House, 1995.

Chapter 2

Power to Spare

BASED ON MARK 5:1–15, 19
KEY VERSE *"And they come to Jesus, and see him that was possessed with the devil, and had the legion, sitting, and clothed, and in his right mind: and they were afraid" (Mark 5:15, KJV).*

OPENING PRAYER
Father God, as I explore the power of Christ over the spirit world, help me to be eager to share my deliverance experiences with others so that they, too, can come to know You as Lord and Savior and glorify You. Amen.

WORDS TO CONSIDER
1. SEA OF GALILEE (MARK 5:1). This sea is noted for its fierce storms which occur because the Sea of Galilee is situated in a rather deep basin between high mountains on the east and a range of hills on the west. The winds rush down the gorges between the hills and sweep over the water, whipping it into high waves and causing severe storms.
2. TOMBS (vv. 2–3, 5). These tombs were cave-like openings cut into the limestone hillsides. Because they contained dead men's bones, they were considered unclean by the Jews. However, lepers, demoniacs, and other social outcasts dwelled in the tombs. Today in Palestine, these places are still used as shelter by Arab refugees and very poor people.

INTRODUCTION
Almost everybody in America knows of superheroes—Batman, Superman, Spiderman, and the Transformers. Today, many children have added the Power Rangers, Iron Man, or the Hulk to their collection. These are figures larger than life, which come to save the day from some evil force. We have a tremendous fascination with them. Moviemakers and comic book publishers make millions of dollars each year from adults as well as children by cultivating an interest in these figures. The super characters appeal to a basic desire in all of us—the desire for power. Much of our literature and folklore, as well as our philosophical writings, is built on this basic urge.

The desire for power forms the basis of our economic and cultural life, as well as, more obviously, our political life. Consequently, we still admire the powerful. Millionaires who amass huge fortunes, when asked why they keep working every day even though they already have more than they will ever spend, sometimes reply that they love the sense of power that money gives them—power over their destiny and over the lives of others.

In chapter 2, the miracles performed by Jesus illustrate the unlimited power of God. Jesus performed these miracles not only to back up His claim that He is the Son of God, but to show us how, through faith in Him and His Word, we can plug into this limitless power.

SCRIPTURE TEXT

MARK 5:1, KJV And they came over unto the other side of the sea, into the country of the Gadarenes. **2** And when he was come out of the ship, immediately there met him out of the tombs a man with an unclean spirit, **3** Who had his dwelling among the tombs; and no man could bind him, no, not with chains: **4** Because that he had been often bound with fetters and chains, and the chains had been plucked asunder by him, and the fetters broken in pieces: neither could any man tame him. **5** And always, night and day, he was in the mountains, and in the tombs, crying, and cutting himself with stones. **6** But when he saw Jesus afar off, he ran and worshipped him, **7** And cried with a loud voice, and said, What have I to do with thee, Jesus, thou Son of the most high God? I adjure thee by God, that thou torment me not. **8** For he said unto him, Come out of the man, thou unclean spirit. **9** And he asked him, What is thy name? And he answered, saying, My name is Legion: for we are many. **10** And he besought him much that he would not send them away out of the country. **11** Now there was there nigh unto the mountains a great herd of swine feeding. **12** And all the devils besought him, saying, Send us into the swine, that we may enter into them. **13** And forthwith Jesus gave them leave. And the unclean spirits went out, and entered into the swine: and the herd ran violently down a steep place into the sea, (they were about two thousand;) and were choked in the sea. **14** And they that fed the swine fled, and told it in the city, and in the country. And they went out to see what it was that was done. **15** And they come to Jesus, and see him that was possessed with the devil, and had the legion, sitting, and clothed, and in his right mind: and they were afraid.

5:19 Howbeit Jesus suffered him not, but saith unto him, Go home to thy friends, and tell them how great things the Lord hath done for thee, and hath had compassion on thee.

BIBLE BACKGROUND

Commentaries tell us that "Gerasa," the town of the demonic man, was in the area of the Decapolis, a league of 10 cities—most of them built by Alexander the Great. This was a predominantly non-Jewish area.

It is also important to note that a "legion" included 4,000 to 6,000 troops. Thus, this man is possessed by a large number of demons that "probably outnumbered the pigs" (Keener 1993).

EXPLORING THE MEANING
1. POWER OVER FORCES OF THE DEVIL (MARK 5:1–15)

After showing Himself to be the master of the physical world by speaking to the waves and the wind in a storm that arose on the Sea of Galilee (Mark 4:35–41), Jesus showed His great power over the spirit world. As Jesus came off the ship onto the shore, He met a man with an unclean spirit who lived in the tombs outside the village. This man wore no clothes; in his frenzy, he tore them off. He was completely uncontrollable. Neither fetters (shackles) nor chains could hold the man because the demons inside him gave him superhuman strength.

According to our lesson, the man was a menace to himself and to others. He lived in the hills—lonely, miserable, crying, and cutting himself with sharp stones. Another version of the story, as recorded in Matthew, says that this man was also dangerous to others. He was so fierce that "no man could pass that way" (Matthew 8:28). In both versions the man needed someone to help him; he could not help himself.

This poor man is a picture of humanity without God. Without Him, we are all potentially dwelling places for evil spirits. Some Bible scholars believe that when we willfully persist in sin, we can become victims of demon possession. Our modern society often experiences the overwhelming pain of sinful nature.

Society tries over and over again to control the destructive evil forces in the hearts and minds of men through the chains of human laws and restrictions. There are many laws against theft, murder, rape, assault, arson, and violence of every kind; but people still commit crimes. Humanity continues to break forth into adultery, sadism, homosexuality, economic exploitation, drug addiction, and alcoholism.

Like the poor man in our lesson, people all around us continue to cry day and night. Many of us have troubles that cause us to cry out in our spirits, and some people are so unhappy that they commit suicide. But Jesus hears our cries and will help us, just as He helped the demoniac in the Gadarenes. No one else can really help us.

When they saw Jesus, the demons in the man were struck with fear (Mark 5:6–7). They recognized Jesus and ran to worship Him. The demons did not worship Jesus because they loved Him, but because they feared Him. They knew that Jesus had power to cast them into hell. Demons do not have faith. They simply have knowledge of who God is because He is Spirit. Jesus would not accept their worship. He wants men who have faith in Him to worship and praise Him out of hearts of love.

Jesus commanded the demons to come out of the man (Mark 5:8). He gave them permission to go into the swine grazing nearby (v. 13). The pigs immediately rushed down a steep hill to the sea, jumping off the ledge until all had drowned. The man who had been tormented with the unclean spirits was completely delivered. The herdsmen of the swine saw what happened and went into the town to spread the news (v. 14). When the people came out to see for themselves, they saw the former demoniac quietly sitting down with Jesus and the disciples, dressed, and fully restored to his right mind (v. 15). The people of the city and surrounding area were seized with fear by the miracle and begged Jesus to leave the neighborhood. He did as they asked.

Jesus is sensitive to our desires. Though He has power to perform the miracle of salvation, He does not do so without our permission. If we ask Him to depart, He will go away and leave us to our own devices. Later, because He loves us, He comes again to knock on our heart's door and gives us another chance to accept His gift of salvation.

2. POWER TO WITNESS (v. 19)
What love and gratitude this freed man must have felt for his deliverer! Jesus had done for him what no one else had been able to do. It should not have surprised anyone that the man now wanted to go with Jesus. But Jesus had a more important task for this man. He told him, "Go back to your friends. Tell them what happened to you."

It was probably difficult for the man to go back and live among the people of the village. Everyone knew the terrible things he had done. Perhaps they would not accept him. Perhaps they would shun him for fear he would become violent again. Perhaps they would even blame him for the loss of the swine and try to kill him. No doubt all these thoughts ran through his mind.

God helps us to live a good life (a life glorifying Him) among our friends. Christ's presence with us gives us joy and victory. Although we worship in His presence, however, we need to always remember that the rest of the world also needs our witness. Perhaps the man in our story went home and did the job Jesus gave him to do. The Bible records that later when Jesus came to this area He received a tremendous welcome. Were these same people who had wanted Jesus to leave their neighborhood now so interested in His message that they remained with Jesus three days while He preached to them (Matthew 15:29–39)?

POINTS TO PONDER

One of the attributes of Almighty God is His omnipotence: He is all-powerful. He is so powerful that He is able to confront unclean spirits and win. Believers must always remember that we are no match for Satan alone. However, Satan is no match for Jesus in us.

REFLECTIONS

1. Meditate on Matthew 5:14–16: *"Ye are the light of the world. A city that is set on an hill cannot be hid. Neither do men light a candle, and put it under a bushel, but on a candlestick; and it giveth light unto all that are in the house. Let your light so shine before men, that they may see your good works, and glorify your Father which is in heaven."* Then answer these questions: How can I let my light (life) shine in a crisis so that God is glorified? What are some of the benefits for Christians who let their lights shine before others?
2. Think of one event in the last three days where you let the light of Jesus shine through you. How did you feel? How would you describe that time to others?
3. Should those who have done something good for the Lord expect that deed to be followed by a blessing from Jesus?

DECIDING MY RESPONSIBILITY

PERSONAL

Write on a sheet of paper or in the study guide at least one thing that needs to be done in your life but you are powerless to do. Then, select a Scripture that assures you that Christ can perform your miracle. Meditate on that Scripture in your daily devotions as you talk to God about His Word. Continue to expect God to keep His promise to you.

COMMUNITY

Ask God to allow someone to cross your path with whom you might share a testimony of God's deliverance. Then, engage in a time of prayer with that individual, asking God to meet that person's need.

CLOSING PRAYER

Thank You, God, for the insights from Your Word. Help me to always remember that You are the all-powerful God and there is nothing that is too hard for You. Amen.

SOURCES

Keener, Craig S. *The IVP Bible Background Commentary, New Testament.* Downers Grove, IL: InterVarsity Press, 1993. p. 147.

Strong, James. *Strong's Exhaustive Concordance of the Bible.* Libronix Digital Library System. Logos Bible Software. Woodside Bible Fellowship, 1996.

The NIV Study Bible. Barker, Kenneth. Grand Rapids, MI: Zondervan Publishing House, 1995.

Chapter 3

The Man of Compassion

BASED ON MARK 5:35–43
KEY VERSE: *"As soon as Jesus heard the word that was spoken, he saith unto the ruler of the synagogue, Be not afraid, only believe"* *(Mark 5:36, KJV).*

OPENING PRAYER

Lord, as I explore Your power in action through this Bible study, help me to embrace Your ability and willingness to come alongside me in my times of need. As I discover anew Your miracles, help me also to determine not to be afraid in times of crisis but to believe in the power of God. Amen.

WORDS TO CONSIDER

1. RULER OF THE SYNAGOGUE (MARK 5:35). The "ruler" of the synagogue was one of two officials selected by the elders to officiate during the activities of the synagogue. The other official was the "minister" or "attendant." The primary duty of the ruler of the synagogue was to take charge of the public worship and to maintain order.
2. TUMULT (vv. 38). "A noise or uproar of persons wailing, of a clamorous and excited multitude, or of riotous persons, as in a breach of public order" (Strong 1996).

INTRODUCTION

On any given day, newspaper headlines reveal the crises that our society faces: an Amber Alert for a missing child, or a neighborhood or city devastated by the damage and death toll of an unexpected storm or an unfettered fire. In any moment, we might each face a personal crisis: a frightening medical diagnosis, or a call that a family member has been in an accident. In the midst of our crises, time may seem to stand still and our thoughts lead us to fear the worst. Only in the power of Christ can we find hope.

In a crisis, it is pretty hard to imagine any human having the power to alter a natural event like death. However, in our Scripture lesson, we encounter Jesus—truly human and truly God, the only One with the power to make a dead person live. As you engage this story, notice Jesus' actions carefully. In His actions with Jairus's daughter, we find the confidence to face the crises of our lives. In His time on earth, Jesus brought the physically dead to life again. As we observe this truth in action, let us also remember that Jesus alone can raise those who are spiritually dead to new life in Him. All they have to do is believe on the Lord Jesus Christ as their Savior, and they will be saved from eternal damnation—separation from a Holy God forever and ever (John 3:16). When we are raised to new live in Him, Jesus has assured us that as Christians we can use His power to successfully confront our critical situations (John 14:12).

SCRIPTURE TEXT

MARK 5:35, KJV While he yet spake, there came from the ruler of the synagogue's house certain which said, Thy daughter is dead: why troublest thou the Master any further? **36** As soon as Jesus heard the word that was spoken, he saith unto the ruler of the synagogue, Be not afraid, only believe. **37** And he suffered no man to follow him, save Peter, and James, and John the brother of James. **38** And he cometh to the house of the ruler of the synagogue, and seeth the tumult, and them that wept and wailed greatly. **39** And when he was come in, he saith unto them, Why make ye this ado, and weep? the damsel is not dead, but sleepeth. **40** And they laughed him to scorn. But when he had put them all out, he taketh the father and the mother of the damsel, and them that were with him, and entereth in where the damsel was lying. **41** And he took the damsel by the hand, and said unto her, Talitha cumi; which is, being interpreted, Damsel, I say unto thee, arise. **42** And straightway the damsel arose, and walked; for she was of the age of twelve years. And they were astonished with a great astonishment. **43** And he charged them straitly that no man should know it; and commanded that something should be given her to eat.

BIBLE BACKGROUND

During Jesus' ministry, He encountered many instances where the people involved felt powerless. One of the most illustrative examples is contained in Mark 5:35–43. In this portion of Scripture, Mark aimed to report the extraordinary nature of Jesus' power. Also, Mark sought to chronicle the astonishment of those who witnessed the power of Jesus. The account in Mark 5:35–43 immediately follows the healing of the demoniac from the Gadarenes. (See Chapter 2—*Encountering Jesus: A Life-Changing Look at the Son of God.*) Because of the notoriety Jesus received from the healing of the man in the tombs, the crowds following Him grew.

Mark tells us that Jesus and the disciples left Decapolis and traveled by ship across the Sea of Galilee, where they were met by a throng of people. In the crowd was a man named Jairus. No doubt people moved aside to let this leader of the local synagogue move to the front of the gathering. Mark says that Jairus saw Jesus and immediately fell at His feet, explaining that his daughter was near death. Jairus's plea was that Jesus would accompany him to the child's deathbed and there "lay thy hands on her, that she may be healed; and she shall live" (Mark 5:21–23, KJV).

In the biblical account, Mark narrates Jesus' ability to confront even death. In the case of Jairus's daughter, death posed itself as an unconquerable foe, challenging any man or woman without a deep and unrelenting faith in God. However, death was no match for Jesus who is 100 percent God and 100 percent man. He is able to be any believer's all in all.

EXPLORING THE MEANING
1. JESUS FACES A CRISIS SITUATION (MARK 5:35–38)
Jairus, the rabbinic leader, and his household found themselves in a crisis situation. While Jesus was on His way to Jairus's house to help Jairus's daughter who was gravely ill, someone from the leader's household met him with the horrendous news. "Thy daughter is dead: why troublest thou the Master any further?" With these words, the messenger not only delivered bad news; he destroyed hope. Everyone, particularly Jairus, was overcome with grief, but Jesus sought to console them by stating, "Be not afraid, only believe" (v. 36). In these words, Jesus spoke hope into the seemingly hopeless situation. Jairus's faith in the midst of his crisis had brought Him to Jesus. Now Jesus' words aimed to restore that faith in the midst of doubt, despite the situation.

When Jesus, with three of His disciples and Jairus, arrived at Jairus's house, they saw friends and loved ones overcome with grief. Mark's narration indicates that many "wept and wailed greatly" (v. 38). The onlookers felt that the young girl's life was at an end, and there was nothing anyone could do to change it.

2. JESUS USES HIS POWER (vv. 39–41)
Humanity's most fearsome enemy is death. Jairus and the members of his family recognized this fact and were crushed by it. They saw death as an inevitable foe that they were powerless to address. They viewed death as inevitable—like the strong waves and winds of sea storms, they could expect it, perhaps brace for it, but never escape it. However, Jesus knew He had power over death and assured Jairus's household that "the damsel is not dead but sleepeth" (Mark 5:39). Knowing that the child was indeed dead, these mourners viewed Jesus' words as absurd. They therefore scorned and ridiculed His comments.

In response, Jesus took only three of His disciples, Jairus, and Jairus's wife into the girl's bedroom. Notice the gentle power with which Jesus operated. Mark writes that Jesus took the girl by the hand. The term "took" seems to imply a light touch, yet the Greek word (*krateo*) means to seize with masterful power. Jesus further demonstrated His power over death when He declared, "Talitha cumi. . .Damsel, I say unto thee, arise" (v. 41).

3. JESUS OBSERVES UNBELIEF (v. 42–43)

The girl immediately arose and walked (v. 42). This was no process over time. Consider that she had obviously been ill for a while and that the messengers had declared her death to Jairus while he was with Jesus. Time lapsed also as Jesus brought the ruler and others to Jairus's house. This was a miracle, fully performed and fully formed on the girl. She arose with the power and ability to walk.

Those who witnessed the miracle of the dead girl being raised to life exhibited unbelief. We caught a glimpse of their unbelief when Jesus alluded to the girl's death as sleep (Mark 5:39). When Jesus suggested that He had power over death, they thought Jesus was joking. However, when His words were backed by miraculous action, those who watched the miracle in unbelief displayed "great astonishment." Though we are left wondering why Jesus instructed the observers of the miracle not to publicize it (v. 43), it is apparent that everyone in the city witnessed that the dead girl was now alive and well.

POINTS TO PONDER

What crisis situation has made you feel as though there was nothing anyone could do? In times of crisis, why is it so important that believers know the promises of God? How can knowing these promises help a believer to be a *victor* instead of a *victim*?

REFLECTIONS

One of the reasons that we study and meditate on God's Word is so that we will know how He wants us to live. Jesus is able to address our crises, but He expects us to also share our knowledge of His power with others. How do you think meditating on God's Word helps us carry out the "Great Commission"? How does it help us to build His kingdom?

Reflecting on your personal meditation in God's word can be helpful in your personal development and in your ability to witness to others. Make a chart that shows when you study and how much time you spend in God's Word during each meditation period. As you review this assessment of your personal devotion time, ask the Holy Spirit to reveal how you might improve in your study of God's Word. Knowing Him strengthens you in times of crisis and in sharing Him with others.

DECIDING MY RESPONSIBILITY

PERSONAL

In times of need, you can use Scripture references to encourage yourself in the Lord. As you read your Bible, write in a journal or on a sheet of paper those Scriptures that can encourage you in crisis situations. Commit to taking these Scriptures into your heart as a way of strengthening yourself in God's Word.

COMMUNITY

Remember that how believers act during a crisis is also a witness to a lost and dying world. At those times, others should still be able to see Jesus in us. They should be able to see our faith in our Lord and Savior in action. Look around you: There are many who have fallen subject to their circumstances. They feel helpless and hopeless. You can show them that their Creator loves them and cares about their needs. Use the Scriptures to encourage someone else in the Lord. Share with them that Jesus can be a very present help in their times of need as well.

CLOSING PRAYER

Thank You, Lord, for helping me to learn so much about Your love and care for humanity. Please help me to be an instrument used by You to comfort others in their times of need. Amen.

SOURCES

Gilbertson, James. *PC Study Bible for Windows* version 2.1C. Seattle: Biblesoft, October 1996.

Strong, James.*Strong's Exhaustive Concordance of the Bible* in *Libronix Digital Library System: Logos Bible Software.* Libronix Corporation. Ontario: Woodside Bible Fellowship, 1996.

Chapter 4

Deliverance and Forgiveness

BASED ON MATTHEW 9:1–8
KEY VERSE: *"But when the multitudes saw it, they marvelled, and glorified God, which had given such power unto men"* *(Matthew 9:8, KJV).*

OPENING PRAYER
Lord, we thank You for your mighty healing power and Your gentle touch. Your deliverance of us from our various places of pain and suffering is a blessing. Thank You for granting us the ability to "arise and walk" even in the midst of suffering. Thank You in the name of Jesus. Amen.

WORDS TO CONSIDER
1. PALSY (9:2, 6). Paralysis (Pfeiffer, Vos, and Rea 1975).
2. BLASPHEME (v. 3). An intentional and defiant dishonoring of the nature, name, or work of God through word or action (Pfeiffer, Vos, and Rea 1975).

INTRODUCTION
The Charles Dickens classic *A Tale of Two Cities* begins with one of the greatest opening paragraphs in literature:

> "It was the best of times, it was the worst of times...it was the season of Light, it was the season of Darkness...we had everything before us, we had nothing before us...in short, the period was so far like the present period..."

How the events of the novel were viewed depended on the perceptions of people. For the aristocrats, it was the best of times, "a season of light" with everything before them. For the peasants, it was the worst of times, "a season of darkness" with no hope before them.

During the time of Jesus' ministry on earth, people responded to the miracles that they witnessed in various ways. They responded by being joyous, or sometimes by being upset. Although it may seem to be a wonderful time to celebrate when a miracle was performed that helped people and changed their lives for the good, people did not always want to celebrate with thanksgiving. For example, Jesus performed two different healing miracles in the cities of Gadara and Capernaum. In Gadara, Jesus delivers two men possessed by demons. In Capernaum, Jesus heals a paralyzed man. The response He received in each city was very different.

The people's reactions to Jesus depended on their viewpoint. The people of Gadara appear to be more materialistic; they feared Jesus and begged Him to leave their city. The people of Capernaum received Jesus and praised God for His power. Our study in this chapter will focus on the miracle and the encounter Jesus had with the people who lived in Capernaum.

SCRIPTURE TEXT

MATTHEW 9:1 And he entered into a ship, and passed over, and came into his own city. **2** And, behold, they brought to him a man sick of the palsy, lying on a bed: and Jesus seeing their faith said unto the sick of the palsy; Son, be of good cheer; thy sins be forgiven thee. **3** And, behold, certain of the scribes said within themselves, This man blasphemeth. **4** And Jesus knowing their thoughts said, Wherefore think ye evil in your hearts? **5** For whether is easier, to say, Thy sins be forgiven thee; or to say, Arise, and walk? **6** But that ye may know that the Son of man hath power on earth to forgive sins, (then saith he to the sick of the palsy,) Arise, take up thy bed, and go unto thine house. **7** And he arose, and departed to his house. **8** But when the multitudes saw it, they marvelled, and glorified God, which had given such power unto men.

BIBLE BACKGROUND

Jesus had completed His teachings to the people about the kingdom of heaven. In His message, which we call the Sermon on the Mount (Matthew 5:1–7:28), Jesus explained that true blessedness is the result of inner character and not external circumstances. He contrasted the outward demonstration of religious practice and the inward practice of righteous living.

After finishing His teaching session, Jesus demonstrated His authority to utter such profound teachings by performing miracles. He performed nine miracles, which fall into three groups. Three were miracles by healing:

the healing of man with leprosy (Matthew 8:1–4), the healing of a Roman soldier's servant (vv. 5–13), and the healing of Peter's mother-in-law (vv. 14–17). Three were demonstrations of His authority: the calming of the storm (vv. 23–27), His power over demons (vv. 28–34), and His forgiving of the paralyzed man, which demonstrated His power over sin (9:1–8). Finally, there were three miracles of restoration: the restoration of the ruler's daughter's life (vv. 18–26), the restoration of sight to two blind men (vv. 27–31), and the restoration of speech to the man who was deaf (vv. 32–33).

Jesus' power, authority, and compassion for others are strong and real. This chapter study provides us with more examples of how Jesus touched the lives of others as He transformed lives and created opportunities for new life.

EXPLORING THE MEANING
1. A MIRACLE AT CAPERNAUM (MATTHEW 9:1–2)
The miracle of healing in this passage is also found in two other Gospels: Mark 2:3–12 and Luke 5:18–26. Each Gospel writer narrates the events a bit differently, as might each reporter who covers a news event. The differences have led some commentators to ponder. While we acknowledge the theological debate of how these events occurred, the purpose of this chapter is to explore the power of Jesus and its impact in our lives.

Matthew begins by sharing that Jesus sailed from the Gadarenes, where the healing of the two possessed men took place. Jesus' healing miracle was a blessing for the men, but it was not well received by others. In fact, some of the business owners did not want Him to stay. Jesus does not stay where He is not wanted, so He got into the boat and went back across the Sea of Galilee to Capernaum.

It was in Capernaum that Jesus had established His base of operations. When word spread that He was back in town, a large crowd gathered at the house where He was staying. According to Mark 2:1–2, the crowd was so large that there was no way anyone could enter through the front door. Luke informs readers that among the multitude listening to Jesus preach that day were religious leaders and teachers from throughout all of Israel (Luke 5:17).

All of the Gospel writers agree that as Jesus was preaching, some men approached Him carrying a man on a stretcher (Matthew 9:2). The man suffered from palsy, a disease that caused a gradual paralysis of the entire body. The paralyzed man was unable to help himself, but fortunately he had friends who had enough love for him and enough faith in Jesus to bring him to our Lord for healing.

The details surrounding the healing differ with various Gospel writers. Matthew records that the paralyzed man was brought to Jesus, but describes the incident differently. Mark 2:2–5 and Luke 5:18–19 record that because of the multitude, the men went around to the side and climbed onto the roof. In those days, houses were made of stone with flat roofs created out of dried mud and straw. Digging through the mud, the men opened a hole in the roof large enough for the stretcher. Then they lowered the man on the stretcher through the roof and down to the floor where Jesus was preaching. (See Mark 2:4 and Luke 5:19.) In these accounts, the roof of the house was torn apart and the man lowered into the building to gain entrance to Jesus. Matthew's account provides a quicker contact between Jesus, the paralyzed man and his friends. Matthew does not indicate that the man had to wait for Jesus to recognize him or that a crowd was in the way.

All of the writers make it plain that it was not the faith of the paralyzed man that moved Jesus, but it was the faith of his friends. In response, Jesus spoke to the paralyzed man, "Son, your sins are forgiven." Not all sickness is caused by sin (see John 9:1–3), but apparently this man's illness was caused by some disobedience to God. So before Jesus healed the man's body, He first brought him into a right relationship with God. Forgiving sins is the greatest miracle Jesus ever performed, and it carried a great price—Jesus sacrificing His life.

2. REPROACH AND RESPONSE (vv. 3–6)

The three Gospel writers record the religious leaders who were in attendance. Matthew 9:3 and Mark 2:6 mention only the scribes, while Luke 5:21 indicates that both scribes and Pharisees were present. When these teachers of the Law heard Jesus forgive the man's sin, they did not speak out. Instead they were furiously thinking, *This man is committing blasphemy.* They were right in their understanding that God is ultimately the Great Forgiver of sin. What they did not understand was that Jesus is God in the flesh (John 1:14).

Their spoken words were not necessary. Jesus knew the thoughts of these so-called teachers and asked them why they entertained such evil in their hearts. He questioned them: "Which was easier: to say, 'Your sins are forgiven' or 'Rise up and walk'?" (Matthew 9:5, paraphrased). While each statement would have been impossible for them, both statements were easy for Jesus! His aim, however, was to teach a much greater lesson. He wanted them, as well as the crowd, to know that He was able to forgive sin. Therefore, Jesus said to the man, "Get up, take your stretcher, and go home" (v. 6. paraphrased).

3. CONFIRMATION AND AFFIRMATION (vv. 7–8)

The man's response to Jesus' words provided people with physical evidence of a spiritual reality. Jesus' action proved that His Word was true. If the man was able to walk, it followed that his sins were also forgiven. At the command of Jesus, the paralyzed man immediately got up from the stretcher and went home.

When the people saw the man walk away, they were filled with fear and awe. This stands in stark contrast to the reaction of the religious leaders. The leaders had come to see what was going on and to find ways to accuse Jesus if they felt His presence threatened their power and position in the community. The people, however, came for the physical healing and the healing words of Jesus. As proven by the response of the four friends, the masses were in need of Jesus' message. They saw Jesus' healing and forgiving as divine gifts. The people glorified God, realizing that God had given true authority to the person they saw as a human being.

POINTS TO PONDER
The men brought the man who was paralyzed to see Jesus. Jesus forgave his sins first, and then He called out the evil thoughts of the teachers of the religious law (Matthew 9:3-4). Next, he told the man to get up and go home because he was healed (v. 6). Why do you think Jesus forgave the man and then healed him? In our lives today, do you see or believe that Jesus works miracles in this same order? What real-life examples support your answer?

REFLECTIONS
Jesus' power and love are manifested throughout His ministry in the many encounters that people experienced because of Him. Encountering Jesus could mean that someone would receive a physical, spiritual, or mental healing and transformation. The miracles of healing provided the external or visible signs that Jesus was more than a prophet and that He deeply cared for others.

The men in this Scripture lesson, who carried the stretcher, showed great care. Neither Matthew, Mark, nor Luke say that these men were "friends," but because of what they did, we say that these men were friends to the paralyzed men. They took the time to find Jesus so that their friend would be healed. They truly epitomized going the distance— or an extra mile or two—for someone else. Their examples gives us much to think about:

1. What are the ways that you genuinely show care to others?
2. Why do you think this story of forgiveness and healing (Matthew 9:1–8) comes after the story of deliverance (Matthew 8:24–34)?
3. What would your response be if someone offered to take you to a healing service to receive healing? Why?

DECIDING MY RESPONSIBILITY
PERSONAL

This week, prayerfully examine areas of your life where you may need healing. Take an honest look at your relationship with Christ. If there are areas where Christ does not rule in your life, ask the Lord for forgiveness and strength to begin practicing a new way of thinking and behaving.

You may also want to consider making a scrapbook or writing a song or a poem that you can use when you are feeling separated from God. It will help you feel connected to Him.

COMMUNITY

As members of a faith community, there are many things we can do to encourage those who are in need of healing or who work in a health profession or ministry.
1. Consider sending inspirational cards to persons working in your church's health ministry or in the health professions.
2. Consider planning a festive party for the nursing home residents, their families, and caregivers.
3. Select a medical care facility for teens or adults, and inquire whether there is something you can do as a volunteer.
4. Volunteer at a hospital or nursing home in your area.

CLOSING PRAYER

O Lord, Your kind acts and grace toward us, when others may not care, are blessings. Thank You, Lord, for Your healing words and actions in our lives today and always. In the name of Jesus, Amen!

SOURCE

Gilbertson, James. *PC Study Bible for Windows* version 2.1C. Seattle: Biblesoft, October 1996.

Pfeiffer, Charles F., Vos, Howard F., Rea, John. *Wycliffe Bible Dictionary.* Peabody, MA: Hendrickson Publishers, Inc., 1975. pp. 262, 459.

Strong, James.*Strong's Exhaustive Concordance of the Bible* in *Libronix Digital Library System: Logos Bible Software.* Libronix Corporation. Ontario: Woodside Bible Fellowship, 1996.

Chapter 5

More Than Enough

BASED ON MARK 6:30–44, KJV
KEY VERSE: *"Remember now thy Creator in the days of thy youth, while the evil days come not, nor the years draw nigh, when thou shalt say, I have no pleasure in them" (Ecclesiastes 12:1, KJV).*

OPENING PRAYER
Dear Lord, You are our provider and our way-maker. Thank You for protecting us and caring for us when life seems to keep us down. Thank You for giving us people who will care for us when we are too weak to care for ourselves. In the name of Jesus, we pray. Amen.

WORDS TO CONSIDER
1. PENNYWORTH (MARK 6:37). A penny was equal to a day's earnings.
2. BASKETS (v. 43). Woven or plaited reeds or straw that serve as containers.

INTRODUCTION
When we think about our lives, we realize that many of our problems and concerns center on finances. The possibility of a recession or of economic instability is ever-present on our financial radar. Consider:

- Has your plant or department been shut down or your company moved?
- Are you wondering how you will pay the mortgage, the car note, and the ever-increasing utility bills and still manage to buy food?
- With so many federal funds being slashed, are you asking yourself how your son or daughter will be able to go to college?
- Are you unsure about whether you will be able to start or maintain a retirement fund?

Whether the apprehension stems from the sub-prime mortgage fiasco, out-of-control gas prices, or some yet to be determined financial crisis, the thought of how to make it from day to day is an economic reality that encompasses many households. Having enough money to pay bills, buy gas, or meet medical expenses seems to be a never-ending daily challenge.

With financial need so close to the top of our daily concerns, we must ask if we depend on God to help us make it through. In times of extreme economic turmoil, do we trust God to provide more than enough? Relying on God to take care of us is sometimes difficult from our human perspective because we feel limited in our own abilities or resources. But trusting the Lord does not depend on our resources, but on His.

Jesus gives the blessed assurance that He is always there for us regardless of what the moment is like for us. Waiting on the Lord can be hard, but when we look back over our life-lessons from God, we can see the countless times that the Lord has kept us and provided for us. God does care and God does provide.

SCRIPTURE TEXT

MARK 6:30 And the apostles gathered themselves together unto Jesus, and told him all things, both what they had done, and what they had taught. **31** And he said unto them, Come ye yourselves apart into a desert place, and rest a while: for there were many coming and going, and they had no leisure so much as to eat. **32** And they departed into a desert place by ship privately. **33** And the people saw them departing, and many knew him, and ran afoot thither out of all cities, and outwent them, and came together unto him. **34** And Jesus, when he came out, saw much people, and was moved with compassion toward them, because they were as sheep not having a shepherd: and he began to teach them many things. **35** And when the day was now far spent, his disciples came unto him, and said, This is a desert place, and now the time is far passed: **36** Send them away, that they may go into the country round about, and into the villages, and buy themselves bread: for they have nothing to eat. **37** He answered and said unto them, Give ye them to eat. And they say unto him, Shall we go and buy two hundred pennyworth of bread, and give them to eat? **38** He saith unto them, How many loaves have ye? go and see. And when they knew, they say, Five, and two fishes. **39** And he commanded them to make all sit down by companies upon the green grass. **40** And they sat down in ranks, by hundreds, and by fifties. **41** And when he had taken the five loaves and the two fishes, he looked up to heaven, and blessed, and brake the loaves, and gave them to his disciples to set before them; and the two fishes divided he among them all. **42** And they did all eat, and were filled. **43** And they took up twelve baskets full of the fragments, and of the fishes. **44** And they that did eat of the loaves were about five thousand men.

BIBLE BACKGROUND

For His original audience of first century believers and for us, Mark provides a Scripture lesson that gives a glimpse of Jesus' power not only over nature, but also over our inability to provide when there is very little to work with or give. This miracle is often referred to as the "Feeding of the Five Thousand." Mark 6:30–44 helps us to truly know that little becomes much when it is given to Jesus. The feeding of the 5000 clearly demonstrates Jesus' power and compassion for others. Mark's lesson on how Jesus provided for the 5000 also shows how teaching and caring for one another are essential ingredients for the ministry of God's Word. As noted by some scholars, "Teaching and feeding show that Jesus is the shepherd" (Keck 1994).

The feeding of the 5000 is considered by some scholars to be a turning point in Jesus' earthly ministry. This miraculous provision story is similar to two prominent Old Testament accounts. The first is the feeding miracle by Elisha who told his servants to feed 100 people with 20 loaves of barley bread (2 Kings 4:42–44). The second, and possibly most important, relates to Moses. The Gospel of John records the feeding of the 5000 and emphasizes the connection with the Old Testament account of Moses' instructions during God's feeding of the people in the wilderness (Exodus 16; John 6:14).

John records that Jesus performed this miracle in the springtime—the time of the Passover. This was exactly the time of year that the Jews expected the Messiah to repeat the Old Testament miracle of God feeding Israel manna in the wilderness. The Jews expected a second Moses at a great apocalyptic feast. Despite parallels, the purpose of Jesus miracle was to feed the crowd—physically and spiritually. The more than 5000 onlookers received blessings that only Christ could have given to them.

EXPLORING THE MEANING
1. THE BEGINNING OF THE MIRACLE (MARK 6:30–34)

There are three main characters in this text: Jesus, the disciples, and the crowd. Jesus could see that the disciples were tired, having just returned from ministering (Mark 6:7-13, 30-31). Suggesting they get away for some rest, Jesus and the Twelve left by boat for a quieter place (Mark 6:32). The people apparently anticipated where Christ and His disciples were going and went ahead of them to the shores of Lake Gennesaret on the Sea of Galilee. The people wanted to see and hear Jesus, so they went from one side of the lake to the other to be in His presence. The crowd was already there when Jesus and His disciples landed.

When Jesus met the people who had followed Him to the shores of Lake Gennesaret, He recognized that they had no spiritual leader. Obviously, Jesus and His disciples were not going to enjoy the rest they had planned. Christ was not annoyed; instead He "was moved with compassion" toward the people (v. 34). Jesus used this opportunity to teach these followers.

2. PARTICIPATION IN THE MIRACLE (vv. 35–44)

Mark records that late in the afternoon the people became hungry. When the disciples discovered that the people had nothing to eat, they wanted to send the people away to buy food, but Jesus did not turn the crowd away. He realized that their physical and spiritual needs were very great. Jesus is able to take care of both.

Jesus commanded the Twelve to feed the people. The disciples were dismayed by the number of hungry people. They immediately responded that their money was insufficient for the very large amount of bread that was needed (v. 37). They estimated that it would take two hundred pennyworth to feed the crowd. This was not just one day's wages, but more than six months of wages! They protested against attempting to provide food for everyone because it was neither practical nor probable based on their lack of funds.

Perceiving the helplessness of the Twelve, Jesus asked them to do what He knew they could do—take an inventory of the food available and ask the people to sit down in groups. The disciples brought the two fish and five loaves of bread to Jesus, and then disciples asked the people to sit in groups of 50 and 100. According to the Gospel of John, the miracle feeding occurred on the green grass in Bethsaida (John 6:10) by the Sea of Galilee (v. 1). The desert setting, however, is not the desert with sand that we may think of, since the people were asked to sit on the green grass. Nevertheless, this open space provided no option for food other than what the Master would provide.

Jesus' directions suggest three important questions. The first question is, "What do you have?" Jesus knew how much food was available, but He wanted the disciples to determine how much they had. Jesus knew that physically they would not have much to feed the people; however, He would be able to provide "more than enough" to care for the multitude and the disciples with some left over!

The second question is, "What do you need?" The disciples took inventory. They knew how much food they had. What they did not know was how much food they needed, but they were sure they needed more than what they had. When the disciples told Jesus how much food was available, they did not ask Jesus to explain or discuss with them how He would feed so many with so little. The disciples simply gave the two fish and five loaves of bread to Jesus and waited for Him to act. The disciples understood even more that Jesus had authority and power.

The third question is, "When do you need it?" Note that the disciples did not ask for food until food was needed. And Jesus met the need when the need occurred. We need to remember that God's time is not always fast, and He may not work things out in the way we prefer or expect.

3. THE MESSAGE OF THE MIRACLE (vv. 30–44)

Now Jesus did what only He could do. The other Gospels all say that there were 5,000 men fed. However, Matthew 14:21 also indicates that only the men were counted, but women and children were also present. Jesus took food, which would otherwise normally feed only a few people, and fed 5,000 men plus women and children. He took the time to care for thousands of people and their need for physical food, human care, and spiritual nourishment.

The food that Jesus used (fish and bread) was common food. The Bible has promised that those who trust God will be fed (Psalm 23; 37:3; Matthew 6:31–33). This promise is not for a feast, just food. But Jesus gives us the opportunity to experience more than enough not only for ourselves but also for others who can be taken care of by what we have to offer. In this case, the disciples were instructed to satisfy the hunger of the people and to show them a miracle from the Lord. This multiple blessing had benefits that would reach deep inside hearts and minds.

There were 12 baskets full of food left after the feeding of the 5000 plus. Sometimes Jesus Christ does not supply just enough; He is "able to do exceeding abundantly above all that we ask or think" (Ephesians 3:20). The phrase "more than enough" applies to our lives as well. When we ponder the three questions posed by this lesson, we can experience this miracle anew. Have you taken inventory of what you have, or do you find it easier to say what you do not have and to focus on what you want? Do you know how much you have? Regardless of the circumstance, this is a question that can be applied to any area of our lives. Finally, are you asking Jesus to supply needs you think you will have in the future? We usually prefer not to wait on God and may even display a lack of patience and a "hurry it up, now" attitude that resembles a 2-year-old's temper tantrum.

Like the disciples, we must learn to follow the leading of Jesus. The miracle is His to perform. Certainly, in those times, we will know assuredly that our blessing is not only for us. God will give more than enough so that there will be a blessing on those we can serve.

POINTS TO PONDER

Do you need a "supply" miracle? Have you taken inventory of what you have? Do you know what and how much you have? Have you brought what you have to Jesus? Have you *asked* Jesus to supply whatever you need? "Ye have not, because ye ask not" (James 4:2). Has the time to meet the need arrived? "Rest in the LORD, and wait patiently for him" (Psalm 37:7).

REFLECTIONS

Think about your relationship with Jesus and your expectations of Him. Now, think about what expectations Jesus has for you in your life as you answer the questions below.

1. Does Jesus ever expect us to do something He knows we cannot do?
2. Are you asking Jesus to explain to you how He will meet your need?
3. Do you ask Jesus to supply needs that you *think* will occur in the future?
4. Are you upset, jealous, or disappointed when God blesses others with the blessing that you needed?
5. Can you name a time when Jesus used you to benefit others? What were your thoughts and feelings?
6. Have you ever seen an adult Christian have a temper tantrum (e.g., sulking, pouting, not wanting to change, not wanting to be helpful, being bitter, giving someone the silent treatment)? What advice might help the person work things through?

DECIDING MY RESPONSIBILITY
PERSONAL

1. Has God ever given you more than you asked Him for? Share that account with at least two people who do not already know your experience.
2. If you cannot think of a time when God has given you "more than enough," meditate on God's Word as you "count your blessings" and circumstances through the years. Record your impressions and then reconsider where God blessed you financially, physically, emotionally, or spiritually.
3. Meditate on Mark 6:30–44 during the next few days, and then share it with at least two people this week.

COMMUNITY

While financial need seems overwhelming, Jesus still expects us to reach out to others.

1. Get involved with a church ministry that provides service for those who are incarcerated.
2. Become a mentor for a child who may need assistance with clothing or homework, or who needs a role model.
3. Help raise money to send a child in need to a summer camp or on vacation.

CLOSING PRAYER

Dear Jesus, You are our way-maker, and Your compassion for us is overflowing. You love us and care about us even when things seem hopeless in our lives. Thank You, Jesus, for helping us to hear your Word and trust You to provide us with what we need in our times of concern. Thank You, Lord, for providing food for those who are hungry and giving us the opportunity and hearts to care for those who are in need or neglected. In the name of Jesus, we pray, Amen.

SOURCES

Keck, Leander E. *The New Interpreter's Bible—New Testament Articles. Vol. III.* Nashville, TN: Abingdon Press, 1994. p. 630.

Keener, Craig S. *The IVP Bible Background Commentary.* Downers Grove, IL: InterVarsity Press, 1993. p. 822.

The NIV Study Bible. Barker, Kenneth, general editor. Grand Rapids, MI: Zondervan Publishing House, 1995. pp. 1489, 1530.

Chapter 6

What Manner of Man is This?

BASED ON MARK 7:31–37
KEY VERSE *"And he charged them that they should tell no man: but the more he charged them, so much the more a great deal they published it"* (Mark 7:36, KJV).

OPENING PRAYER
Lord, I pray that You would open my ears to let me hear You, my eyes, so that I may see You, and my heart, so that I may receive You in all that I do, say, and think. In the name of Jesus, I pray. Amen.

WORDS TO CONSIDER
1. TYRE (MARK 7:31). A Gentile city located in Phoenicia (modern Lebanon), which bordered Galilee (*The NIV Study Bible* 1995).
2. SIDON (v. 31). A city approximately 25 miles from Tyre. Both Tyre and Sidon were "proud, historic centers of Canaanite paganism with tombs of ancient kings and temples of Melqart/Heracles, Asarte, and various other deities" (*The NIV Study Bible* 1995).
3. DEAF (v. 32). Those in whom the sense of hearing is nonfunctional for the ordinary purposes of life (Riekehof 1978).

INTRODUCTION
Whether it is during the hot and highly humid summer, or in cold and bone-chilling winter, we will hear reports of persons who die from weather-related conditions: no air, overheated, no heat, or homelessness. Tragic stories abound of young and elderly persons who die because they are exposed to extreme temperatures. Newspapers and the nightly news programs highlight stories about death or tragedy. These are among the personal stories that remind us that pain is very real. These problems are vast. They occur around the world and give both Christians and non-Christians reasons to ask, "Why is there so much suffering in the world today?" or "Why do people experience pain?"

We can gain some insight by studying the Old Testament. In Job we see Job move from accepting the tragedies in his life to becoming a man who tells God what he really thinks about his afflictions and horrendous troubles. God's response to Job's complaining is found in Job 38 through 41. God pointedly gives Job a detailed reality check regarding who He (God) is and the wonderful blessings that He has given to Job. This reminder keeps Job from thinking that God has been unfair and unjust with him.

If we are going to question God about our struggles and sorrows, we must also question our moments of joy, happiness, fun, and laughter. The two questions—"Why pain?" and "Why joy?"—must be asked together in order to get a balanced perspective on life. For balance, therefore, we must have hope: the hope that is embodied in the Person of Jesus Christ, the Son of God, the Master Teacher, the Divine Healer.

SCRIPTURE TEXT

> **MARK 7:31** And again, departing from the coasts of Tyre and Sidon, he came unto the sea of Galilee, through the midst of the coasts of Decapolis. **32** And they bring unto him one that was deaf, and had an impediment in his speech; and they beseech him to put his hand upon him. **33** And he took him aside from the multitude, and put his fingers into his ears, and he spit, and touched his tongue; **34** And looking up to heaven, he sighed, and saith unto him, Ephphatha, that is, Be opened. **35** And straightway his ears were opened, and the string of his tongue was loosed, and he spake plain. **36** And he charged them that they should tell no man: but the more he charged them, so much the more a great deal they published it; **37** And were beyond measure astonished, saying, He hath done all things well: he maketh both the deaf to hear, and the dumb to speak.

BIBLE BACKGROUND
In this study, the Gospel writer, Mark, shares another powerful healing miracle of Jesus. In this case, the miracle immediately impacts both the life of the person who receives the blessing and those around him. Mark is the only Gospel writer to tell about this man who was deaf and whose speech was impeded. Jesus' approach to healing in this instance is very physical. We also find that Jesus takes the man away from the crowd, adding a different dynamic to His public ministry.

Mark's style in revealing this miracle indicates that Jesus was in touch with the customs of the people He was ministering to in the area of Sidon. Historically, these people believed that human spittle or saliva had a curative quality. Although Jesus has all power, He was sensitive to the beliefs of the people in the area. Therefore, Jesus' use of spit as medicine brings enlightenment to the traditional customs of the people.

Mark's fast-paced writing style allows us to see several miracles of Christ as His ministry expands beyond the Israelites. Through Mark's writing, we view the compassion of God for all, and we learn the importance of our caring for others and bringing them to Jesus regardless of what state they are in, so that their lives, too, can be transformed.

EXPLORING THE MEANING
1. THE PLACE (MARK 7:31)
Location is important in the Gospel accounts. It is through the geographical footprint of Jesus that we chronicle His ministry and the spread of the Gospel's hope. Mark, whose narrative takes us quickly through the geography of Palestine, tells us that this particular account is set in Decapolis. In Chapter 2, the miracle of deliverance of the demoniac, who lived in the tombs, also took place in Decapolis, the non-Jewish area composed of a league of 10 cities built by Alexander the Great.

Tyre and Sidon were major sister cities, seaports located on the Phoenician coast, and the site of many Old and New Testament accounts. Tyre is located in area of Phoenicia which bordered Galilee. Sidon was some 25 miles away from Tyre. Together they were one of the major centers of Canaanite worship.

2. JESUS' COMPASSION (vv. 32–35)
Mark's writing is filled with movement and excitement. It actually has the feel of a modern action film, with quick and clear images that drive home the most important points. But unlike modern films which have action for the sake of action, Mark's writing demonstrates the compassion and concern of Jesus. Mark's language declares the urgency of the need and the necessity of Jesus' response: "And they bring unto him one that was deaf, and had an impediment in his speech; and they beseech him to put his hand upon him."

Somebody was sensitive to the deaf man's plight and decided to take him to see Jesus. Like the friends or family in this text, we do well to bring people to Jesus through the medium of prayer. When we encounter those who are in need of divine healing, our task is not to evaluate their worthiness, question them, judge them, or check their credentials. Our assignment is to bring people to Jesus. He can help them.

Jesus showed tenderness and consideration for the man. We can only imagine that Jesus might have put His arm gently around the man's shoulder or lightly guided him by touching his arm. One scholar speculates that Jesus may have shown through His actions the words "healing," "speech" and "from God" to let the man know what He was about to do. The Jewish Law acknowledged that deaf persons could use signs to communicate (Keener 1993). Whatever method Jesus used, we know that communication was made despite the man's hearing and speech conditions. Jesus' compassion for this man was evident. We, too, must take the time to show compassion and care to others.

When the man was brought to Jesus, Jesus did something we do not generally see. Usually when Jesus went to a person or someone was brought to Jesus for healing, the actual act of healing occurred before the growing throngs. However, in this case, Jesus took the man away from the crowd. Some scholars believe that Jesus' choice not to perform the miracle "before all the people" was a humble response, indicating that Jesus did not seek His own glory and teaching us to avoid being ostentatious (Abraham 1994).

After moving the man away, Jesus put His fingers into the man's ears (v. 33). This seems to indicate that the main issue was the man's hearing. The most important thing, perhaps, is being able to hear the voice of the Savior so that we might respond. As Psalm 40:6 records, "Sacrifice and offering thou didst not desire; mine ears hast thou opened." Psalm 78:1 states, "Give ear, O my people, to my law: incline your ears to the words of my mouth." It is our open attention to the Word of the Lord that leads us to understand His desire in our lives. Jesus' placing His finger in the man's ear gave a sense of the necessity and order of the life that is attentive to Christ.

Next, Jesus "spit, and touched his [the man's] tongue" (Mark 7:33). Spittle or saliva was believed to have healing power. While we generally think today of spittle as being unclean, let us not forget that saliva contains our DNA, our genetic make-up. This was the spit of Jesus—while all human, He was also all God. If the ancient culture of Tyre believed spit was medicinal, what more healing could there be than in that which Jesus gave of Himself?

Jesus touched the man's tongue. The man was said to have had a speech impediment of some sort. We cannot be sure if he could speak at all, if he only made utterances, or if his speech was not understandable. Whatever the case, Jesus' touch of the man's tongue seems to indicate that, if the main thing was hearing the voice of the Lord, the next thing would be responding. The word "touched" is translated from the Greek *haptomai*, which implies clinging to something or entering into a relationship with someone. Jesus did not timidly touch the tip of the man's tongue. He seems to have grasped it, perhaps feeling "virtue" or power (*dunamis*) go out from Himself as it did when the woman with the issue of blood touched (*haptomai*) the hem of His garment (Mark 5:30)

In addition to spitting and touching the man's tongue, Jesus looked "up to heaven and sighed." Jesus would never let it be thought that He was not working the work of His Father. His upward look seems to confirm that it is the Father's will that is being done. In confirmation, then, Jesus says to the man *Ephphatha,* which meant "be opened" (v. 34). Jesus makes His connection with heaven and God the Father as He lifts up His eyes, and then tells the man who was deaf and who could not speak that his ears and his voice were not locked anymore. The man immediately began to speak and everyone could hear him.

Given the location of this miracle, it is unlikely that the man who was healed was Jewish. In that case, the meaning of the man's healing opens up a larger picture for us to consider. The healing would then be "symbolic of a more general restoration of hearing and speech" which "confirms that the kingdom of God and the movement of renewal" is extended beyond Israel (Coogan 2001).

3. THE RESPONSE (vv. 36–37)

Despite Jesus' attempt to leave the crowd, the crowd must have found Him. After the miracle, Jesus told the people not to tell anyone but, of course, the people did not listen (Mark 7:36). Although the people did not keep quiet, Jesus' compassion and care were not diminished. Jesus opened the ears and the voice of a man who had friends or family that believed in Jesus. Their belief, the man's willingness to be healed, and Jesus' healing power and compassion are a testimony to the love of Christ.

Seeing a man who was deaf suddenly made able to hear and speak probably created so much excitement and joy in the people that they were unable to contain themselves. It is hard to keep quiet when something so wonderful and spectacular has occurred. Jesus had changed an impossible situation into a memorable moment. He had given the man and the people around him an amazing experience. The power of God had provided this man with a different outlook on life. In so doing, others witnessed what God can do.

It is impossible to read this miracle account without being reminded that we must witness to others about the love of God. The Holy Spirit can open our ears so that we can be sensitive to the lost, dying, confused, and discouraged people of the world. But dealing with people whose problems are far beyond our capacity to even consider, we cannot foolishly think that such power or the judgment is in our hands. First, we must remember to accept people just as they are. We must neither judge nor prejudge the lives of others. Even in the case of those we know do not know Christ, we must love the sinner despite how uncomfortable we are with the sin. Only then can we can hear the cries of people just as Jesus did.

We would be far less frustrated and anxious in our relationships and service, if we would remember to look to Jesus. That is where our resources are located. Jesus Christ is the source of our strength. There is also one additional lesson to learn from this biblical account which closes on an exciting note—the testimony of the witnesses. Mark declares that they "were astonished, saying, He hath done all things well" (Mark 7:37). This is a solid promise that we can help and offer hope to people who need healing from physical, emotional, and social diseases. God is wonderful and He can heal any problem, issue, or suffering when we allow Jesus to minister through us.

POINTS TO PONDER
Jesus depended on our heavenly Father when He performed the miracles. Think about the first time Jesus performed a miracle in your life. How did you know that your miracle was because of Jesus? When was the last time you told someone about the miracle-performing power of Jesus in the Bible and in your personal life?

REFLECTIONS
1. Share two miracles that you have witnessed in the lives of both a Christian and a non-Christian.
2. There are many needs that call us to be compassionate. Based on this Scripture, what guidelines can we use to help determine how to respond to human needs?
3. Do you think Christians should receive miracles before persons who are not Christians? Why or why not?

DECIDING MY RESPONSIBILITY
PERSONAL
The personal benefit of sharing the compassion of Christ with others cannot be underestimated. The great joy is not in the satisfaction of what you have done, but in the realization of what Jesus can do for others. Consider this list of ideas as a jumpstart-kit for greater engagement in accepting personal responsibility to witness for Christ.

1. Learn hymns or contemporary gospel songs in American Sign Language or Signed English that you can teach to those who can hear and share with persons who are deaf in your church.
2. Develop a ministry or partner with a ministry in your church that provides care for people in need. You might consider participating in a ministry for single parents, organizing a clothing drive, establishing a food pantry, or providing assistance to help people obtain legal representation or housing.

COMMUNITY
Your assistance is needed in many areas in the church and community. Here are a few suggestions that might begin or extend your work in compassion to others.

1. Spend time learning more about foster care. Then assist a family who has embraced foster children with special needs.
2. Seek other ways to help individuals with disabilities or families who are caregivers to person with various needs.
3. Partner with another ministry or volunteer with a local group that supports a camp and/or works with children who are deaf.

CLOSING PRAYER

Lord, thank You for Your goodness and Your mercy toward us each and every day. Thank You for allowing us to enjoy your grace and blessings in our lives. Thank you for caring for us and helping us with what we need. We also want to say thank You for being with us during our times of difficulty and despair. Your mercy and grace are ever before us and are such treasures in our lives. In the name of Jesus, we pray, Amen.

SOURCES

Abraham, A. Kenneth. *The Matthew Henry Study Bible.*Iowa Falls, IA: World Bible Publishing, 1994. pp. 1906-1907.

Barker, Kenneth., ed. *The NIV Study Bible.*.Grand Rapids, IA: Zondervan Publishing House, 1995. pp. 1505-1506.

Coogan, Michael D.*The New Oxford Annotated Bible.* Oxford: University Press. 2001. p. 71.

Keener, Craig S. *The IVP Bible Background Commentary, New Testament.* Downers Grove, IL: InterVarsity Press, 1993. pp. 154-155.

Riekehof, Lottie L.*The Joy of Signing: The Illustrated Guide for Mastering Sign Language and the Manual Alphabet.* Springfield, MO: Gospel Publishing House, 1979. p. 7.

Chapter 7

Jesus: The Light of the World

BASED ON JOHN 9:1–11, 35–41, KJV
KEY VERSE: *"And Jesus said, For judgment I am come into this world, that they which see not might see; and that they which see might be made blind"* (John 9:39, KJV).

OPENING PRAYER
Dear Lord, help me to grasp the significance of Your Word for my life. Give me the spiritual enlightenment I need to recognize your light in my life and commit to Your service as a faithful light to the world. In the name of Jesus. Amen.

WORDS TO CONSIDER
1. POOL OF SILOAM (JOHN 9:7) The word "Siloam" means "one who has been sent." It is "a rock cut-out pool on the southern end of the main ridge on which Jerusalem was built. It served as part of the major water system developed by King Hezekiah" (*The NIV Study Bible* 1995).
2. PHARISEES (v. 40) The name Pharisees means "separated ones." The Pharisees were scribes and lawyers known for their fanatical devotion to the Law, especially the traditions about tithing and purity. Such teaching made it difficult for them to accept Jesus' teachings (Gruen 1998).

INTRODUCTION
One of the things we take for granted is light. We expect to enter a room, flip a switch, and see the space flood with illumination. Light is so important that most of us cannot imagine living without it. With recent calls to save energy, we have changed our bulbs, but we would never consider giving up the comfort and convenience of the light switch!

The same is true of sunlight. Scientists have sounded the alarm, but we ignore the dangers of ultraviolet light and take for granted sunlight we expect each day. We are appalled at any idea that light as we know it, both natural and humanly generated, would ever not be used or not be available for our personal benefit.

The sad thing is that the most important light of all is too often forgotten. That light is Jesus, "the Light of the world" (John 9:5). The light of Jesus Christ illuminates our spiritual path and keeps us from stumbling in the darkness of sin and despair. Only Jesus Christ can help us see where we are and where we need to be in God. Without Jesus, we are spiritually blind, groping in the darkness of sin, unable to find our way through spiritual and often physical turmoil. It is only with the light of Jesus that we can see the path of righteousness, truth, and mercy.

In this text, we will see two contrasting views of people who encounter the "light of the world": those who are physically blind and seek the help of Jesus, and those who are spiritually blind and attempt to forge their own path. Jesus knows both well and has an answer for each.

SCRIPTURE TEXT

JOHN 9:1 And as Jesus passed by, he saw a man which was blind from his birth. **2** And his disciples asked him, saying, Master, who did sin, this man, or his parents, that he was born blind? **3** Jesus answered, Neither hath this man sinned, nor his parents: but that the works of God should be made manifest in him. **4** I must work the works of him that sent me, while it is day: the night cometh, when no man can work. **5** As long as I am in the world, I am the light of the world. **6** When he had thus spoken, he spat on the ground, and made clay of the spittle, and he anointed the eyes of the blind man with the clay, **7** And said unto him, Go, wash in the pool of Siloam, (which is by interpretation, Sent.) He went his way therefore, and washed, and came seeing. **8** The neighbours therefore, and they which before had seen him that he was blind, said, Is not this he that sat and begged? **9** Some said, This is he: others said, He is like him: but he said, I am he. **10** Therefore said they unto him, How were thine eyes opened? **11** He answered and said, A man that is called Jesus made clay, and anointed mine eyes, and said unto me, Go to the pool of Siloam, and wash: and I went and washed, and I received sight.
9:35 Jesus heard that they had cast him out; and when he had found him, he said unto him, Dost thou believe on the Son of God? **36** He answered and said, Who is he, Lord, that I might believe on him? **37** And Jesus said unto him, Thou hast both seen him, and it is he that talketh with thee. **38** And he said, Lord, I believe. And he worshipped him. **39** And Jesus said, For judgment I am come into this world, that they which see not might see; and that they which see might be made blind. **40** And some of the Pharisees which were with him heard these words, and said unto him, Are we blind also? **41** Jesus said unto them, If ye were blind, ye should have no sin: but now ye say, We see; therefore your sin remaineth.

BIBLE BACKGROUND

In John 8, Jesus creates a storm among the leaders and the people by confronting traditional views of sin. He forgives the woman taken in adultery and challenges her accusers regarding their own sin. He also declares publicly that He is the Light of the world and challenges the most sacred claim Jews could make—their kinship to Abraham. The Pharisees understood that Jesus was declaring Himself to be God and the only source of salvation. His remarks caused them to declare Him a liar, deem Him a devil, and pick up stones to kill Him. In their blind rage, they missed His point, and He walked through their midst as He exited the temple.

The Pharisees used the healing of the man born blind as an excuse to accuse and discredit Jesus. The "crime" supposedly was that the miracle had been performed on the Sabbath. In reality, the Pharisees were threatened by Jesus' bold statement regarding His identity as "the Light of the world" (John 9:5). Following that assertion, Jesus healed the man who had been born blind, verifying His declaration. However, to make their effort seem legitimate, the Pharisees initiated a trial to investigate the healing. It began with a question for the parents and then a call for the man to testify. The accusations continued and finally the man was ejected from the synagogue. While such a miracle should have been gladly received, the Jewish leadership found reasons to refuse to see the truth that stood before them.

EXPLORING THE MEANING
1. JESUS IS THE LIGHT (JOHN 9:1–5)

Imagine the streets of Jerusalem as Jesus and His disciples made their way along the crowded corridors teeming with people—beggars, peddlers, the rich, the famous, the infamous, and the needy. In the throng, the eyes of the disciples fell upon the man who had been born blind. Looking from the outside, the man probably appeared to have accepted his condition either as the punishment that others said it was, or the inevitable "hand he had been dealt." Perhaps he had his secret days of self-pity or was tormented by the voices of those wondering about his sinful state. Maybe he had resigned himself to living in darkness. Without sight, the man had taken to begging. With that skill, there probably was such streetwise savvy that no one wondered if he even wanted to see.

The disciples' question (v. 2) regarding the sin that had caused the man's condition was a common one. It was the theological explanation for illness. It was the culturally safe thing to assume and gave people the right to pity the person and thank God that they were not in that condition of sin and illness.

Jesus' response went to the core of the question and upset the status quo: "Neither hath this man sinned, nor his parents" (v. 3). This opened the door to an option never before considered. This deliverance would not be about sin. Jesus declared that through the blindness of this man "the works of God should be made manifest" (v. 3). Jesus' purpose would be fulfilled in this man's situation: "I must work the works of Him that sent me" (v. 4).

It was daylight. The dawn had come. It was time for the manifestation of God's hand to meet this man's destiny to be made whole. But Jesus let the disciples and the passersby know that this opportunity would not last forever: "The night cometh, when no man can work" (John 9:4). But Jesus gave a special assurance: "As long as I am in the world, I am the light of the world" (v. 5). There can be no darkness as long as Jesus is present. There can be no time when the work of the Father cannot be done as long as Jesus Christ shines in the hearts of those who hear His voice and recognize Him as the Anointed One of God.

2. JESUS GIVES SIGHT (vv. 6–11)
Jesus then spat on the ground, made mud with His spit, and placed this concocted eye salve on the man's eyes before telling him to go wash in the Pool of Siloam (vv. 6–7) at the southeast corner of Jerusalem. Several points here are worth noting. First, God's ways are past finding out. A salve made of clay and human saliva would probably have not been the medicine of choice, but when viewed in the context of Jesus' act, we see Him moving in His humanity—represented by spit and clay—to act in His divinity, the miracle of healing.

The second principle, listening to the voice of God, is coupled with the third principle, obedience. The man was not concerned about the presence, doubts, or questions of the crowd. He neither wondered how far it was to the pool nor asked who might see him with his dirty face. He simply "went his way therefore, and washed, and came seeing" (John 9:7). The miracle was instantaneous and obvious. If we—like the man—follow the direction of Jesus, we cannot help but see.

The man's problems began when he encountered his neighbors (v. 8). Unwilling to accept the truth of the miracle, they were so callous that they questioned his identity. But the man was neither too proud nor too timid to confront their doubts with the truth. He eagerly admitted, "I am he" (John 9:9). He was so absorbed with God's mercy, love, and grace that he could not keep it to himself. He did not mind letting everyone know how his life had been changed.

The next question for the onlookers was, "How were thine eyes opened?" (v 10). People search for answers but often will not accept the truth. The man had a limited revelation of Jesus, having only heard His voice once. He was not near Jesus when his sight was restored. Therefore he responded with the only truth he knew: "A man that is called Jesus made clay, and anointed mine eyes, and said unto me, Go to the pool of Siloam, and wash: and I went and washed, and I received sight" (v. 11).

3. JESUS DEFINES SIGHT (9:35–41)
While the man's testimony should have brought praise for God, it caused him to be thrown out of the synagogue by the Pharisees (John 9:24–34). He was at the point of ejection when Jesus again came to the man. The man had given testimony to the miracle of God in his life. While he did not know the man who had sent him to the pool, he knew that he once was blind but now could see.

Jesus, therefore, asked the man about the source of his belief: "Dost thou believe on the Son of God?" (John 9:35). Knowing that the Son of God was the only One who could have performed the miracle, the man admitted that he doesn't know Him but wants to believe (Gk. *pisteuo*). Once Jesus enlightened him spiritually, the man worshiped Him (vv. 37–38).

Jesus then revealed His role as the One who came to judge the world, to reveal the hearts of people, and to shed light where darkness had reigned. Jesus explained Himself by using a metaphor drawn from the blind man's miracle. Those who thought they had sight would be made blind by the truth of His doctrine or teaching. Those who were blind by human standards would be able to see because of the illuminating presence of Jesus (John 9:39).

Jesus did not reveal Himself to the man in some dark and remote alley. There were Pharisees standing near who overheard Jesus and wanted to know if He was calling them "blind." Actually, they wanted to know if Jesus was calling them sinners. Jesus' response was that if they accepted Him as Savior as the man did, they would not be blind to the truth. Because they rejected Him, their sins would remain, and they would have the greater condemnation.

Jesus is indeed the Light of the world. He shed light into the life of the blind man and caused the man to praise God even in the face of powerful opposition. He shines His light in our hearts so that no sin separates us from the love of God. Jesus is the Light. Aren't you glad?

POINTS TO PONDER
1. What situation have you faced that you did not readily see as a miracle and instead chose to question the possibility of the events before you?
2. When God begins to enlighten us, we can expect opposition. What opposition are you facing because of the light of Jesus in your life? What light is Jesus shedding through this Bible study that can strengthen you in facing that opposition or challenge?

REFLECTIONS

1. Sometimes we find ourselves resigned to situations believing that we are getting our due because of our bad choices or circumstances that are beyond us. Think about an area of your life where you are resigning yourself rather than seeking God's will and direction. How can you take the concern to Jesus so that He can give you new vision?

2. Can you recall a time when God directed you even though you were blind or unclear about His identity? How did that time impact your life? How have you now come to know Him?

DECIDING MY RESPONSIBILITY
PERSONAL
While our humanity has pitched us into the darkness of doubt and dread, the salvation of Jesus has made a way out of no way and shed light in our lives. Begin to count your blessings. List ways and times that Jesus has shed light in your spiritual blindness.

COMMUNITY
Like the man born blind who was given sight, we must take on the commitment to share the Light of Christ with the world. As those who have received the Light of Jesus Christ, we must shine hope into the despair that others experience. What blindness do you see in your community? What light can you shed in those situations?

CLOSING PRAYER
Lord, thank You for caring enough to deliver me from spiritual blindness. Help me to have a new understanding of this Bible text so that, like the man born blind, I too can share the source of light with others. In the name of Jesus, Amen!

SOURCES

Gruen, Dietrich. *Who's Who in the Bible*. Lincolnwood, IL: Publications International, Ltd., 1998. p. 436.

Life Application Study Bible (King James Version). Wheaton, IL: Tyndale House Publishers, Inc., 1996. pp. 2071–2073.

Strong, James. *Strong's Exhaustive Concordance of the Bible*. Libronix Corporations: Logos Bible Software. Ontario: Woodside Bible Fellowship, 1996.

The NIV Study Bible. Barker, Kenneth, general editor. Grand Rapids: Zondervan Publishing House, 1995. p. 1611.

Chapter 8

Confrontation in Jerusalem

BASED ON MARK 11:8–10, 15–19, 27–33
KEY VERSE: *"And they that went before, and they that followed, cried, saying, Hosanna; Blessed is he that cometh in the name of the Lord"* (Mark 11:9, KJV).

OPENING PRAYER
Dear Lord, I thank You for demonstrating that courage is necessary in order to take a stand for God. Impart to me wisdom so I can stand in the face of opposition and confrontation in ways that bring honor to You. In the name of Jesus, we pray. Amen.

WORDS TO CONSIDER
1. HOSANNA (MARK 11:9–10). "Save us." It is a quotation from Psalm 118:25.
2. TEMPLE (vv. 15, 27). The central place of worship in the Jewish faith. The temple was only located in Jerusalem. The temple in the time of Jesus was called Herod's Temple. Solomon's Temple had been destroyed during the Babylonian captivity. Community discussion of the Torah or Law took place in local synagogues.
3. MONEYCHANGERS (v. 15). A collection of bankers who sat in the temple and charged a fee to exchange Roman coins for Jewish or temple coinage. They also sold animals for the temple sacrifice.

INTRODUCTION
"Confrontation" is a word that can be counted on to send people running in opposite directions. When James Forman and other civil rights workers tried to be served at segregated lunch counters in the South, that confrontation sometimes ended with bloody faces. Confrontation is usually not easy. It requires us to reach into the deep emotions of our hearts and minds. It demands that we put things on the line.

Generally, there is a purpose for honest confrontation. For Forman and others, it was civil rights and freedom for Black people. Something that important could not be passed over and neglected. True, there were risks to life and limb, but human dignity and the exercise of personal freedom were more important.

In this lesson, we will see how Jesus deals with confrontation. At the beginning of His ministry, Jesus' miracles and authoritative teaching were received with popular enthusiasm. But when Jesus began to address unpopular issues like sin and purity in the house of God, the trouble started. The scribes and Pharisees could not take the piercing critique that Jesus brought to the religious establishment. Confrontation became inevitable.

SCRIPTURE TEXT

MARK 11:8 And many spread their garments in the way: and others cut down branches off the trees, and strawed them in the way. **9** And they that went before, and they that followed, cried, saying, Hosanna; Blessed is he that cometh in the name of the Lord: **10** Blessed be the kingdom of our father David, that cometh in the name of the Lord: Hosanna in the highest.

11:15 And they come to Jerusalem: and Jesus went into the temple, and began to cast out them that sold and bought in the temple, and overthrew the tables of the moneychangers, and the seats of them that sold doves; **16** And would not suffer that any man should carry any vessel through the temple. **17** And he taught, saying unto them, Is it not written, My house shall be called of all nations the house of prayer? but ye have made it a den of thieves. **18** And the scribes and chief priests heard it, and sought how they might destroy him: for they feared him, because all the people was astonished at his doctrine. **19** And when even was come, he went out of the city.

11:27 And they come again to Jerusalem: and as he was walking in the temple, there come to him the chief priests, and the scribes, and the elders, **28** And say unto him, By what authority doest thou these things? and who gave thee this authority to do these things? **29** And Jesus answered and said unto them, I will also ask of you one question, and answer me, and I will tell you by what authority I do these things. **30** The baptism of John, was it from heaven, or of men? answer me. **31** And they reasoned with themselves, saying, If we shall say, From heaven; he will say, Why then did ye not believe him? **32** But if we shall say, Of men; they feared the people: for all men counted John, that he was a prophet indeed. **33** And they answered and said unto Jesus, We cannot tell. And Jesus answering saith unto them, Neither do I tell you by what authority I do these things.

BIBLE BACKGROUND

Jesus and His disciples were making their way to Jerusalem. They passed the towns of Bethany and Bethphage. These towns were located near the Mount of Olives, just east of Jerusalem, an area known for its figs and dates. It is no wonder that Bethany means "house of dates" and Bethphage means "house of unripe figs." Bethphage is "located on the East slope or ridge of the Mount of Olives on or near the Jericho-Jerusalem road" (Pfeiffer, Vos, and Rea 1975). Bethany was the home of Lazarus and where he was raised from the dead.

The ultimate destination in this text is the Temple in Jerusalem. Two words are used in New Testament Greek for "temple." One (Gk. *naos*) means "sanctuary," the Holy Place. Access to this area was limited to the priest. However, in Mark 11:15, the word used is *hieron,* which means "sacred place" and refers to the entire vicinity of the temple. More specifically, it refers to the temple courts, an area of about 25 acres. The Court of the Gentiles was the outermost court and the largest section of this area. It was here that sheep, oxen, and doves were kept and sold for use as sacrifices. It was also in this section of the temple that Roman coins were exchanged for Jewish coins. It was in this Gentile court area where Jesus began to cleanse the temple.

The Sanhedrin was headquartered in Jerusalem. This religious ruling body was composed of 70 members and a president. These men were drawn from three classes of Jewish society: the chief priest, the scribes, and the elders (Matthew 16:21, 27:41; Mark 8:31, 11:27). The Sanhedrin had been given authority by the Roman government over all legal and social codes of the day. Their primary tasks were to address local Jewish disputes and to oversee the temple. They confronted Jesus about His credentials in a typical rabbinic dialogue, but Jesus beat them at their own game.

EXPLORING THE MEANING
1. ENTERING JERUSALEM (MARK 11:8–10)

Mark 11:1–7 sets the context of our lesson passage. Prior to entering Jerusalem, Jesus dispatched His disciples to bring Him a donkey. He then entered the city riding the donkey. Note that the disciples were obedient to the Lord despite the "strange" set of instructions He gave them.

Clearly, Jesus' choice of a donkey and His entire journey down the Jericho Road into Jerusalem was the fulfillment of the prophecy: "Rejoice greatly, O daughter of Zion; shout, O daughter of Jerusalem: behold, thy King cometh unto thee: he is just, and having salvation; lowly, and riding upon an ass, and upon a colt the foal of an ass" (Zechariah 9:9).

In short, Jesus was consciously presenting Himself to the Israelite people as their king, their Messiah. It is little wonder then that the Gospels give a royal flavor to this triumphant event. The spreading of garments and palms along Jesus' path was a sign of the highest honor and praise (Luke 19:36; John 12:13). This jubilant event was also marked by the cries of "Hosanna! Hosanna!" The people blessed Jesus and rejoiced in the prospect of the kingdom of David coming. (It is this entry of Jesus into Jerusalem that we acknowledge on Palm Sunday.) But while "Hosanna" or "Save now" was the cry, Jesus knew that the moment of praise would not last long. Very soon, possibly some of these same people would be shouting "Crucify him; crucify him" (Luke 23:21).

2. CLEANSING THE TEMPLE (11:15–19)

After the event that is commonly called the "Triumphal Entry" into Jerusalem, Jesus made a visit to the temple. Matthew gives us the impression that His visit happened on the same day as His entry, but Mark shows it was on the next day (Mark 11:12).

The outrage Jesus displayed would today be called "righteous indignation." Jesus was no coward, nor was He a physical weakling. As He moved through the temple area turning over tables, people knew that Someone significant was at work.

We should understand, of course, that Jesus was not in the "sanctuary" of the temple, but in the court area. In the Gentile court, animals and birds were bought and sold for sacrifices. Worshipers had to exchange coins that had pagan deities on them or that were minted at Tyre in order to give their offering in the temple. If they had not exchanged their coins, they would have violated the commandment against making any graven images as recorded in Exodus 20:4. Various vendors would sell the animals used during the time of sacrifice.

Jesus' outrage was anchored in the Scripture that He apparently quoted as He stormed through the temple: "My house shall be called the house of prayer; but ye have made it a den of thieves" (Matthew 21:13). It was this sharp indictment that provoked the scribes and chief priests to plan Jesus' assassination (Mark 11:18).

3. CONFRONTATION WITH THE SANHEDRIN (vv. 27–33)

Jesus left the city after His dramatic clearing of the temple, but He did not stay away. When He and His disciples returned to the temple courts, He was met by the members of the Sanhedrin. In verses 17 and 18 of our text, we learn that these men had started to plot a way to destroy (Gk. *apollumi*) Jesus. The most obvious way would be a "legal" indictment. The encounter here is aimed at setting the legal precedent for discrediting and even killing Jesus.

The motive was fear (Mark 11:18). The religious leaders knew, as demonstrated by the Triumphal Entry, that Jesus had a large following—mostly poor people—who probably applauded the scene at the temple where they had likely been extorted for years under the guise of worship. In the minds of the chief priest and scribes, Jesus had to be stopped.

In typical establishment fashion, they questioned Jesus' credentials: "Who gave thee this authority to do these things?"(Mark 11:28). Can you imagine the absurdity of these feeble men questioning the authority of the Son of God? Jesus' work, like that of John the Baptist, was authorized in heaven. It was divine and not of human origin. If the Sanhedrin members knew this, they were not about to acknowledge such authority in either Jesus or John. Their only response was that they just didn't know how to answer Jesus' question. Their excuse, however, was inadequate. They sought not to recognize the truth of God but to maintain political status, personal safety, and social position.

In these verses, Jesus not only faced confrontation but He made sure that those who were opposing divine direction were challenged to recognize God's plan. As Mark presents this segment of the chronicles of Jesus' life, he confirms the life-changing nature of confrontational encounters with Christ. Jesus has every right to do His work in our world and our lives. And He will do it—with or without our approval.

POINTS TO PONDER
While we reflect upon the interactions of Jesus and the Sanhedrin, we must remember that we challenge the Lord's authority when we choose to follow our own path or to ignore the clear mandates of His Word. Reflect on the times in your life when you have been confronted by the Word of God. How did you respond? What lesson did you ultimately learn about the authority and kingship of Christ?

REFLECTIONS
1. The concern or question about having fundraisers in the church is sometimes a hot topic among Christians. Think about how Jesus reacted in the temple and the background information about the reasons why moneychangers where in the temple. Use this information and your own experiences to consider if this passage only applies to those who went to the temple in Jesus' day. Does it apply to church fundraisers today? Why or why not?
2. What impact should Jesus' indignation have on the church today? Does it? Why or why not?

DECIDING MY RESPONSIBILITY
PERSONAL
Even as He was approaching the city, Jesus wept over Jerusalem because they rejected His offer of salvation and He knew judgment was coming (Luke 19:41–42). Have you ever wept for a city? Has your heart ever been broken by seeing the tragedy of masses of people confused and blinded by Satan and on their way to a certain destruction? Consider

Jesus' emotional response to this situation, and then examine your own responsibility for compassion and action on behalf of those who need to know Christ.

COMMUNITY

Should the religious establishment be confronted when there is evidence of the abuse of God's people? Consider this text from the standpoint of how Jesus' earthly ministry, anchored in Scripture, as He was moved to set God's people free rather than allowing them to continue in the bondage of greedy leaders. What reform is needed in your community or the larger Christian community to release those who are vulnerable to forms of religious charlatanism and abuse?

CLOSING PRAYER

Lord, help me to honestly honor You as my King and Lord. Strengthen me to be bold in confronting injustice as it conflicts with the truth of Your Word. Give me the wisdom to stand for You. I pray in Your name. Amen.

SOURCES

Beitzel, Barry. *The Moody Atlas of Bible Lands.* Chicago: Moody Press, 1985. pp. 164, 172–73.

Douglas, J.D., editor. *The New Bible Dictionary.* Grand Rapids, MI: Eerdmans Publishing Company, 1962. pp. 578, 857, 1230.

Meyers, Rick. *e-Sword,* version 7.6.0. Franklin, TN. http://www.e-sword.net/ 2000-2005.

Pfeiffer, Charles F., Vos, Howard F., and Rea, John. *Wycliffe Bible Dictionary.* Peabody, MA: Hendrickson Publishers, 1975. p. 226.

Chapter 9

The Risen Christ Commissions Disciples

BASED ON MATTHEW 28:1–10, 16–20, KJV

KEY VERSE: *"Go ye therefore, and teach all nations, baptizing them in the name of the Father, and of the Son, and of the Holy Ghost: Teaching them to observe all things whatsoever I have commanded you: and, lo, I am with you always, even unto the end of the world. Amen"* *(Matthew 28:19–20, KJV).*

OPENING PRAYER
Dear Lord, as I study Your Word, help me to be sensitive to the power of Your Resurrection. Help me understand its importance, not only for the first-century witnesses but also in my personal life and in my contribution to Your kingdom. In the name of Jesus, we pray. Amen.

WORDS TO CONSIDER
1. MARY MAGADELENE (MATTHEW 28:1). Mary Magadelene was a devout follower of Jesus. He had cast out demons from her. Mary was from the city of Magdala, and she was one of the first persons to tell of the Resurrection of Jesus.
2. SEPULCHRE (v. 1). A burial place for persons of "importance and wealth" (Youngblood 1995).

INTRODUCTION
Imagine that you are at the bedside when a dear friend passes from this world. At the funeral, you speak of the good life your friend had in Christ. Your words bring real comfort to the family. At the gravesite, you watch as the casket is lowered into the ground and the preacher pronounces the final words.

A few weeks later, you go back to the gravesite alone. With flowers in hand, you approach the grave but find it open and the casket empty. A man dressed in a bright white suit suddenly appears and explains that your friend is alive.

How do you think you might feel? What would you do? Would you run and tell someone or keep the occurrence to yourself, believing that you had finally "lost it"? In essence, this is the dilemma found in this Scripture text and in each of our lives when we realize that Jesus is not dead; He is alive!

SCRIPTURE TEXT

MATTHEW 28:1 In the end of the sabbath, as it began to dawn toward the first day of the week, came Mary Magdalene and the other Mary to see the sepulchre. **2** And, behold, there was a great earthquake: for the angel of the Lord descended from heaven, and came and rolled back the stone from the door, and sat upon it. **3** His countenance was like lightning, and his raiment white as snow: **4** And for fear of him the keepers did shake, and became as dead men. **5** And the angel answered and said unto the women, Fear not ye: for I know that ye seek Jesus, which was crucified. **6** He is not here: for he is risen, as he said. Come, see the place where the Lord lay. **7** And go quickly, and tell his disciples that he is risen from the dead; and, behold, he goeth before you into Galilee; there shall ye see him: lo, I have told you. **8** And they departed quickly from the sepulchre with fear and great joy; and did run to bring his disciples word. **9** And as they went to tell his disciples, behold, Jesus met them, saying, All hail. And they came and held him by the feet, and worshipped him. **10** Then said Jesus unto them, Be not afraid: go tell my brethren that they go into Galilee, and there shall they see me. **28:16** Then the eleven disciples went away into Galilee, into a mountain where Jesus had appointed them. **17** And when they saw him, they worshipped him: but some doubted. **18** And Jesus came and spake unto them, saying, All power is given unto me in heaven and in earth. **19** Go ye therefore, and teach all nations, baptizing them in the name of the Father, and of the Son, and of the Holy Ghost: **20** Teaching them to observe all things whatsoever I have commanded you: and, lo, I am with you always, even unto the end of the world. Amen.

BIBLE BACKGROUND

Despite the fact that Jesus repeatedly spoke about His death, no one expected His Resurrection! His disciples felt they had lost a good friend and prophet. They had been convinced that He was the Promised One, the Messiah, and the One who would deliver Israel from political oppression. But the events of Jesus' trials and the cruelty of the Crucifixion triggered persecution and left Jesus' followers in fear. The disciples had slipped into mourning and collectively found themselves settling into the reality of what would follow for them now that Jesus was gone. The men were probably focusing their attention on recent events with the soldiers, the

Roman government, and the crowds. The women were preparing to anoint Christ's body inside the tomb—the final resting place.

It was customary as a means of honor to prepare the body of the deceased with spices. Since Jesus probably died late in the day prior to the Sabbath, preparation had to wait. Early on Sunday, the women found themselves walking the distance alone to complete the task that only they could do—anoint the body according to custom. The women described here are Mary Magdalene and Mary, the mother of James and Joseph (Matthew 27:56).

The actions of the guards are not cited in our passage, but they are important. Realizing that their lives were in danger both because they had failed to "secure the area" and that the knowledge of Jesus' power would surely spark a revolution, the soldiers went to the leaders with their report. Matthew reports that what followed were bribes, lies, and a cover-up to the highest levels of government and religious leadership (Matthew 28:11–15).

EXPLORING THE MEANING
1. THE WOMEN COME TO THE TOMB (MATTHEW 28:1–8)
The women, who ministered to Jesus, had watched the events of His crucifixion and death from afar (Matthew 27:55–56). When they arrived at the tomb, other events had already been put into motion. It is unclear whether these events occurred simultaneously, but they were certainly a spiral of events. First, there was an earthquake that shook the gravesite as the angel of God opened the grave. The Roman guards, having experienced the tremor and the resulting flashes of light, became so afraid that they seemed petrified as if they were dead.

Just as we might be amazed and slow to take in the events of an automobile accident as it occurs, the women had much to consider. The grave was opened. The massive stone that had been used to secure the spot was moved out of place. Their first thought was not of the stone but of the grave. Their next thought would have been for Jesus, who had been in the grave.

At this point, the women saw the angel who sat atop the massive stone. The appearance of the angel was like nothing the women had seen before. The popular Bible paraphrase *The Message* describes the angel's countenance in Matthew 28:3 by stating, "Shafts of lightning blazed from him."

The angel's words addressed their three main concerns. First, the angel caused them to look away from their fears to the hope that he held. Then he addressed their fear. He told them that he knew why they were there and that the fear they were experiencing was anchored in the fears that had escalated since the Crucifixion. Finally, he said that he had the proof they needed to answer all of their questions. While they, like us, had to trust God by faith, the angel let them know that God was not going to withhold the proof of His power from them. The women were led to the empty tomb where the angel gave instructions that they should go to tell the others.

The women left with mixed emotions. They were afraid. The Greek word *phobos* is the root of the English word "phobia." Their fear was far from normal. They were gripped by fear, petrified by unreasonable possibilities, plagued by doubts and concern. On the other hand, they had great joy. The Greek word for "great" is *megas.* In other words, they had mega-joy! Excited, they ran to share this word from God! (Strong 1996).

2. MEETING THE RISEN JESUS (vv. 9–10)

What could be better than to know that Jesus is alive? What joy the women must have had at the anticipation of seeing Jesus in Galilee! And then, what was good got better. There before them was Jesus. In the midst of their obedience, Jesus showed up. In the middle of their emotional roller coaster, they had this encounter (Gk. *apanteo*). This was no vision, no mirage brought about by the heat or the sun. This was Jesus, who in a reassuring word spoke to them. His greeting "All hail" is translated from the Greek word *chairo,* which means literally to be "full of cheer" and "calmly happy." With a word, Jesus swept away concern and doubt. He moved aside questions and issues. He calmed the anxiety of their hearts the same way He had calmed the waters in the midst of turbulence (Matthew 8:26).

The women responded the only way they could—they worshiped Him. These women, who had anticipated so much and seen their world turn upside down and back again, fell prostrate (Gk. *proskuneo*) before him, reached out, held His feet, and worshiped the Lord they loved. Jesus then repeated the words of the angel, speaking calm into their hearts, sending them to the disciples with the word that He would meet them in Galilee.

3. COMMISSIONED BY CHRIST (vv. 16–20)

The Eleven knew the spot! They went to Galilee to the mountain where Jesus was to meet them. Matthew's eyewitness account seeks not only to communicate the historic event but also to communicate the revelation of the Messiah into history. Theological speculation abounds given Paul's reference in 1 Corinthians 15:6 that the Resurrected Jesus was "seen of above five hundred brethren at once"; but we have no idea if others who had followed Jesus in life followed the disciples to Galilee.

Upon meeting Jesus, the Eleven also experienced mixed emotions. The disciples also fell prostrate before Him and worshiped Jesus. Yet, Matthew reports that there was doubt in some hearts. Who doubted and why?

Remember that the Resurrection was not anticipated. Matthew, in his honesty as a witness and writer, leads us into the midst of the emotional range these Eleven experienced. Perhaps they had wondered if Jesus would reveal Himself to them as He had to the women. Maybe they wondered if this would indeed be Jesus. After all, no such experience ever occurred before.

Despite the doubts, they worshiped when Jesus revealed Himself. Their spirits knew the truth of God's promise, which stood before them. The Greek indicates that some were hesitant; they did not understand. They did not grasp the full meaning or the implications of these events. Still, they trusted their faith, they trusted Jesus, and they worshiped.

Like the women who had reached out to Jesus immediately, the Eleven apparently fell prostrate before Jesus. Verse 17 explains that Jesus then came to them and spoke. How marvelous to consider that when we can't seem to get close enough, Jesus comes in our hour of doubt, hesitation, and fear. He spoke not just a word of peace but a word of power.

Jesus declared to the disciples that He had "all authority" in both heaven and earth. His authority encompasses the entire universe and serves as encouragement to all believers. The Eleven were then told that by this same authority, Jesus was empowering them to "teach all nations." Literally, Jesus commissioned them to "make disciples of all nations" (Matthew 28:19, NIV). These men, unlearned and unknown aside from their relationship with Jesus, were being told to "make disciples" and "to teach all nations." These who had just been afraid to leave Jerusalem were now told to "go into all the world." Jesus knew that they did not know what to do. They had not seen themselves as leaders, as those who were worthy in any way of having "followers." So Jesus explains the discipleship program: baptize and teach. The promise of Matthew 28:20 rings true today as it did in A.D. 30: "Lo, I am with you always."

Christ will be with the church and individual believers as He was with those who walked with Him, those who had been His inner circle. Jesus Christ will be with us to love us, to comfort us, and to empower us so that we can fulfill our assignment of witnessing to and discipling others. Like the women and the Eleven who encountered Jesus in His full Resurrection power, we, too, are instructed to go into all the world—beyond our families, beyond our neighborhoods, beyond our cities and towns.

Matthew has shared the story of Jesus' life on earth, His death, and His Resurrection; but we know that the Gospel is not concluded in these verses. Instead, it is being fulfilled by the presence of the living Christ in the midst of His church, in the lives of the twenty-first century disciples who have been commissioned by the Risen Christ.

POINTS TO PONDER

What range of emotions, memories, and questions might have flooded the women's and disciples' minds?

REFLECTIONS

When did you decide that Jesus was alive? Share your revelation with someone. Include those words and images that come to mind and help you tell about Jesus being alive in your life.

DECIDING MY RESPONSIBILITY
PERSONAL

Some people debate whether Jesus is alive. They argue that there is a division between Jesus, the man, and Jesus, the Resurrected Christ. Their summation is that Jesus is physically dead but the "Spirit of Christ" is alive today. Considering the encounters of this lesson and the witness of Paul in 1 Corinthians 15:6, what would be your personal response to such doubt?

COMMUNITY

Violence, poverty, greed, unwed pregnancy, suicide, and murder are on the rise. Popular culture portrays our society as seemingly dead to spiritual virtues and moral understanding. What do you see as the connection between the Resurrection of Jesus and any hope for the resurrection of moral centering in our society? What actions can you engage in that will help fulfill the Great Commission and bring about the societal resurrection you see needed?

CLOSING PRAYER

Dear Lord, thank You for the Good News of Your Resurrection. The events of this lesson have revealed the chain reaction that proves Your work in this world was far from over. It was just the beginning! Help me to embrace the commission You have given me to fulfill Your will in this world. Amen.

SOURCES

P. C. Study Reference Library: Nelson's Bible Dictionary. BibleSoft. http://www.biblesoft.com/.

Strong, James. *Strong's Exhaustive Concordance of the Bible.* Libronix Digital Library System, Logos Bible Software. Libronix Corporation. Ontario: Woodside Bible Fellowship, 1996.

Youngblood, Ronald F., editor. *Nelson's New Illustrated Bible Dictionary.* Nashville, TN: Thomas Nelson,1995. pp. 1260-1261.

Chapter 10

A View of the World that Chronicles Jesus' Life

BASED ON: GENESIS, MATTHEW, MARK, AND JOHN
KEY VERSE: *"All scripture is given by inspiration of God, and is profitable for doctrine, for reproof, for correction, for instruction in righteousness"* (2 Timothy 3:16).

Encountering Jesus: A Life-Changing Look at the Son of God has taken you through the miracles of Jesus as He lived as the Word Incarnate (God in flesh) among the people. Throughout this study, it has been important that each miracle be explained in the context of its time and place as well as in the spiritual journey that our own lives chronicle. Interestingly, we can also view the time and setting of Jesus life from a broader perspective. Each of the Gospel writers developed a narrative that engaged his audience so that they might see Jesus in a way that brought life-changing power to their own lives.

In this chapter, the aim is not to highlight the miracles of Jesus, but to bring to light the power of the Gospels and the impact of the presence of folk of African descent upon the world Jesus encountered.

GENESIS: THE BIBLE'S FOUNDATION

Genesis, which serves as the foundation for the rest of Bible, provides a survey of God's revelation to us from Creation until Israel enters Egypt. Its opening verse begins with God, who out of "void and darkness" created the beginning of life. As the word "Genesis" denotes, there are several beginnings cited in the book of Genesis: the beginning of the earth, the universe, humanity, and animals.

But in Genesis we also see the beginning of sin and the fall of man. The decline and deterioration of humanity came quickly. Genesis 3 conveys how sin and corruption resulted in God expelling Adam and Eve from the Garden of Eden. As a result, the "blame game," murder, death, and evil became fully intermingled with God's world.

The stories of Genesis have continued to move generations. The book of Genesis is filled with stories of families, covenants, and relationships with God and among people. The issues, joys, concerns, and problems of Genesis provide an intriguing and exciting backdrop for an unveiling of God's plan: first in Adam, Eve, and their family, and then through Noah and the generations that came from him. It was during Noah's time that people were so totally immersed in corruption and sin that God destroyed the earth by the Flood, saving only Noah and his family to replenish the earth (Genesis 6–9).

It is through the call of Abraham and his family that we witness the beginning of the Hebrew nation which God used to introduce salvation to the humankind (Genesis 12). Abraham's son, Ishmael, was born to Hagar, the maid-servant of Abraham's wife, Sarah. Hagar gave birth to Ishmael because Abraham and Sarah could not wait on God for a child. They knew the promise of God, but lacked the faith to wait on God. Ishmael was the first born son of Abraham, but was not "the son of Promise." It is not until Abraham's faith is strengthened that we read of the birth of the promised son, Isaac, through Abraham's wife, Sarah.

The line of promise and succession from Abraham's offspring brings us into an understanding of God's chosen family. Isaac, who married Rebekah, had two sons—Jacob and Esau. God selected Jacob to build His nation and receive the blessings that would have customarily gone to Esau, Isaac's firstborn. Jacob had 12 sons and one daughter. It was with these offspring that the book of Genesis ended as Jacob's son, Joseph, was uplifted and blessed by God to bring God's blessing upon the nations.

In Joseph's story, then, the Book of Genesis came full circle. That which started with God's Creation ended with God's favor upon a Jew and Gentile through His chosen vessel of hope. The Jewish nation is represented by Jacob and his sons who come to Joseph seeking food in time of famine. The Gentile world was represented as Joseph administrated God's bounty in a nation that did not know his God. Joseph was a prototype of Christ, the Only Begotten of God, the One whose story is told in the pages of the Bible, the One who is the Word and who became flesh and dwelt among us.

THE IMPACT OF AFRICA ON THE CHRONICLES OF JESUS' LIFE

In seeking to better understand the life of Jesus, it is important that we take at least a cursory look at the presence of Black people in the ancient biblical world. The significance of Africa and the movements of Africans throughout the Bible provides an opportunity for us to learn the identities of those Black persons who helped to shape the Christian world. This snapshot of the many people, places, and times where people of African descent have been engaged in the events of the Gospel record helps us to understand even better the people and events that have shaped our faith today.

The location of Palestine, in the northeast quarter of Africa and on the border of Asia, is presumptive of a Black presence. According to anthropologists, the area was originally populated by people who migrated from Africa possibly between 2,500 to 5,000 B.C. Since then, there has been a continuous Black presence in the area we know as Palestine. By the time of the New Testament, Greeks and Romans had been added to the population, and because of the powerful presence of these nations, we tend to see their presence as predominant and to minimize the presence of other peoples. To do so, however, is to misrepresent the world of the Gospel writers.

The early people of that area were Hamites and Semites. Ham and Shem, along with Japheth, were the three sons of Noah. It is through Ham's line that people of African descent trace their biblical roots. Ham's sons were Cush, Phut, Mizraim, and Canaan (Genesis 10:1, 6). The term *Ham* means "black" or "burnt face." However, it is critical to understand that skin color in biblical days was a non-issue. It is in recent history, since the 1600s, that the racism of mankind has centered on skin color. With this bigotry, the world has been subject to every possible attempt to deny—with pens and pictures—the presence of Blacks in biblical history. The world into which Jesus was cast was not one that discriminated based on such racial lines. To state that Ham's skin was dark is to describe Ham, since the culture would have simply accepted everyone without concern for skin color.

The Bible also reveals the influence of people of color to the story of the New Testament. The apostle John, though born in Palestine, eventually settled in Ephesus. While we do not have access to specific references to the population of Ephesus, we can infer the presence of people of color. We know that the entire Mediterranean world derived much of its knowledge from Africa and specifically from Alexandria, which was built by Alexander the Great. The library at Alexandria held 700,000 books and scrolls, and people from all over the Greek world, including Ephesus, came to Africa to study and obtain their education.

While Ham's line marks the beginning of our understanding of people of African descent in the Bible, the presence of Black people continues throughout this book. Even a partial list of Black people whose lives unfold in the pages of the Pentateuch, can help us understand the prevalence of Blacks in the biblical text.

NIMROD—Nimrod, whose father was Cush, was viewed as "a mighty hunter before the Lord," a king, and a kingdom builder of Babel, Erech,

Accad, and Calneh in Shinar (Genesis 10:8–11).

MIZRAIM OR EGYPT —The name for Egypt, which is located in Africa, is Mizraim. Egypt is the location where the Hebrews were forced into slavery for the Pharaoh for 400 years. It later became the place of refuge for Jesus and His family when they fled to escape Herod (McCray 1990; see also Genesis 10, 12, 13, 15, 21, 25, 26; Matthew 2:13–15).

RAHAB—Rahab was the prostitute of Canaan who hid the Israelite spies (Joshua 2:1-21, 6:17). Canaanites were the descendants of Ham (McCray 1990).

URIAH—Uriah was a Hittite (2 Samuel 11:3, 6). Hittites were the descendants of Canaan, who, in turn, was a descendant of Ham (McCray 1990).

QUEEN OF THE SOUTH—Also known as the Queen of Sheba, she ruled the kingdom of Sheba "located southwest Arabia" (McCray 1990). The people of Sheba were descendants of Cush (1 Kings 10:1, 2; 2 Chronicles 9:1).

CANAANITE WOMAN—This woman lived in the area of the Phoenician cities, Tyre and Sidon near the Mediterranean Sea (Matthew 15:21–28). Canaanites were the descendants of Ham. Phoenicians gave civilization the alphabet and our numbering system. They were noted for their commerce and their inventiveness (*The NIV Study Bible* 1995).

SIMON OF CYRENE—Simon was made to be the "cross bearer for Jesus" (McCray 1990; see also Matthew 27:32). Simon was from Cyrene, which was located on the northern coast of Africa (*The NIV Study Bible* 1995).

ALEXANDER AND RUFUS—The two sons of Simon of Cyrene (Mark 15:21).

THE GOSPEL AND ITS WRITERS: CHRONICLING THE LIFE OF JESUS CHRIST

Overview of the Gospel of Matthew
Matthew, the author of the book known by his name, was initially a tax collector. When confronted with the words of Jesus, Matthew left the tax business to become an apostle of Jesus Christ. The book dates from approximately A.D. 50 or 60. It was written primarily to Jews to show that Jesus is, indeed, their promised Messiah. The frequent statements that events in the life of our Lord were a fulfillment of the Old Testament prophecy affirm the author's intent. However, the Book of Matthew was not intended for Jews only, as the Great Commission makes clear. The Good News of the Gospel should be preached to all (Matthew 28:16–20).

Historically, Matthew's Gospel tells of events that took place after a 400-year span, which begins with the time of Malachi—the last prophet of the

Old Testament—and ends with the appearance of Jesus Christ. Between these points in time, Jews who had returned from the Babylonian captivity lived under the rule of Persians until Alexander the Great conquered the Middle East.

When Alexander died in 323 B.C., his four generals divided his empire among themselves. Palestine became a contested territory that traded hands during wars between the descendants of Generals Ptolemy and Seleucus. The Seleucids were not tolerant of Jewish religion and customs, and attempted to force Greek culture upon the people. One Seleucid ruler, Antiochus IV, even sacrificed a pig on the Jewish altar. This resulted in a bitter guerilla war led by the Maccabees, Jewish rebels who overthrew the Seleucids and set up an independent state in 165 B.C. Ultimately, the Romans conquered Palestine in 63 B.C. Jesus, therefore, was born when Rome ruled not only Palestine, but the entire known world.

The genealogy recorded by Matthew linked Jesus to God's covenant with Abraham, through whose seed God declared all people on the earth would be blessed (Genesis 22:15–18). The genealogy traced Jesus' lineage back through David, the seed of whom God promised would rule forever (2 Samuel 7:12–16; Psalm 89:19–37). Matthew's gospel satisfied its purpose by showing that Jesus is the fulfillment of Old Testament prophecies as a descendant of Abraham and heir to the throne of David.

Matthew introduced Jesus as a legitimate heir to the throne of David. He was worshiped by the Magi, who came looking for the king in Jerusalem. Having been properly introduced, Matthew showed Jesus putting forth His statement of kingdom righteousness in the Sermon on the Mount before He established His credentials by the miracles He performed (Matthew 8–11). Despite the certification of His authenticity as the Son of God, Jesus' popularity provoked opposition from the Jewish leaders (Matthew 12–16:12).

Knowing that He was rejected by the Jewish nation, Jesus prepared His disciples for His rejection, Crucifixion, and death. Jesus formally presented Himself to the nation with the Triumphal Entry (Matthew 21). The leadership of Israel, however, rejected Him and gained the cooperation of Rome in crucifying Him. Jesus' Resurrection on the third day vindicated His claims. Finally, Jesus commissioned His disciples to proclaim the Gospel all over the world (Matthew 28:16–20).

Overview of the Gospel of Mark

Mark, or John Mark, was the son of a woman named Mary and a relative of Barnabas, the companion of the apostle Paul. The name John was his Hebrew name, while Mark or Marcus was his Roman name. The Gospel of Mark was written about A.D. 50 or A.D. 60, shortly after Peter's death and before the destruction of the temple in A.D. 70.

There is no one consensus about the purpose of the Gospel of Mark. Two beliefs are prevalent. First, the idea is that the Gospel of Mark was written primarily to be a witness documenting Jesus Christ as the Son of God. The second theory is that Mark was writing to prepare his readers for the suffering and persecution they faced as first century Christians (*The NIV Study Bible* 1995).

While it appears second in the Christian version of the Bible, the Gospel of Mark is believed to have been the first written Gospel. Early church tradition attests that John Mark was the Gospel's author, and that Rome was its place of origin. The fact that the Book of Mark was clearly written for a Gentile audience is evidenced by the Jewish customs which are explained throughout the text, as well as its use of terms that reflect the Roman way of living. Mark's gospel is filled with very lively events and tells us more about Jesus' actions than His words (*The NIV Study Bible* 1995).

As a young man, Mark traveled with Barnabas and Paul on their first missionary journey to Cyprus (Acts 12:25; 13:5, 13). Because Mark abandoned the team in Pamphylia (Acts 15:38), Paul refused to take John Mark on the missionary group's second journey. Paul and Barnabas argued over the issue and finally parted, going separately on missionary trips. Mark returned with Barnabas to Cyprus, while Paul traveled further into Asia Minor with a new partner, Silas (15:39–40).

Fortunately, Paul's confidence and respect for Mark was regained later in life. Paul told his son in the faith, Timothy, to bring Mark with him on the next visit. Mark "is profitable to me for the ministry," wrote Paul (2 Timothy 4:11). Later church tradition claimed Mark to be the founder of the Christian church in Alexandria, Egypt.

John Mark used sermons preached by Peter as well as accounts of Peter's passionate personality and his very close friendship with Jesus as the foundation for this Gospel. It was the preaching of the Good News by Peter that formed the eyewitness character of Mark's gospel. One scholar has suggested that the fast-moving nature of Peter was reflected in Mark's record of the sermons. Mark's connection with Peter began at an early age through Mary, his mother. It is clear that the apostles and Mary were companions together in the ministry of Jesus because it was her home that Peter visited after his miraculous release from prison (Acts 12:12).

Compared to the Gospels of Matthew, Luke, and John, Mark's Gospel is the shortest and places less emphasis on the teachings of Jesus. For example, Mark provided his readers with fewer parables than are found in Matthew and Luke, respectively. Mark also did not give information about the birth and childhood of Jesus as do Matthew and Luke. Instead, Mark moved quickly from the ministry of John the Baptist to the public ministry of Jesus. Although the Book of Mark has many parables, it also records Jesus' activities with the miraculous including His acts of healing and His confrontation with the Devil.

It is the core of Jesus' mighty acts that form the basic structure of Mark's Gospel. Ninety-five percent of the information found in the Gospel of Mark can also be found in Matthew and Luke. When compared to the other Gospels, Mark's action-packed account of the ministry events and miracles of Jesus provides the readers with a sense of energy and gives a distinct flavor that is particular to Mark's writing style.

Through words like "immediately," the reader knows that Jesus is on the move. Mark's emphasis on the movement of Jesus was reflected in his understanding of Jesus as the Son of God. Mark succinctly packed together the life, death, and Resurrection of Christ in a manner that compromised the "beginning" from which the apostolic preaching in Acts was the continuation.

Overview of the Gospel of John

John, the son of Zebedee, an apostle of Jesus Christ, composed this Gospel in order to encourage belief in Jesus as the Christ, the Son of God. The place of origin for John's gospel appears to be Ephesus. By the time of its writing around A.D. 85 to 90, Jerusalem had been destroyed by the Romans (A.D. 70), and Christians and Jews had been scattered to various sectors of the Roman Empire. The apostles Peter, Paul, and James had been martyred. The conflict between Christianity and the Roman Empire had been accentuated by the philosophy that Roman emperors were to be worshiped as gods. This philosophy was in stark contrast to the Christian teaching that only the transcendent God almighty and His Son Jesus were worthy of worship.

The Roman Empire did not want Christian beliefs or practices to become the dominant way of life or thinking for its people. The attempt by Rome to eradicate Christian thinking can probably be viewed in the same light as Rome's attempt to destroy Greek influence when Rome conquered Greece. Conflict between the Roman Empire and Christianity was so strong that many Christians severely suffered for their beliefs. Persecution and brutal torment were used to deter Christians from holding and practicing their beliefs. Some Christians were burned alive at stakes, given to lions as sport in stadiums, slaughtered with swords, and tortured and killed in a myriad of cruel public actions.

The Gospel of John begins with a prologue (1:1–18) in which John introduced Jesus as the Word that became flesh. John maintained that the Word existed in eternity and in time became human so that those who believe might have life eternal. Through the skillful account of eight selected miracles and the discourses of our Lord, John showed the growing impact of Christ's ministry.

John began by establishing Jesus' identity and existence. He then shared various events in Jesus' life that caused others to intersect, reject, or follow Him. John also spent time in chapters 13 through 17 giving us a window to peer into the relationship that Jesus developed with His disciples as He prepared them for His death, ultimate victory, and ascension. A number of divine titles were ascribed to Christ by others and affirm His deity: the Lamb of God, the Vine, the Shepherd, the Door, the Water of Life, Bread from Heaven, Son of God, the Way, the Truth, and the Life, and the Resurrection.

SOURCES

Barker, Kenneth, ed. *The NIV Study Bible.*. Grand Rapids: Zondervan, 1995.

Life Application Study Bible (King James Version). Wheaton, IL: Tyndale House Publishers, Inc., 1996.

McCray, Walter Arthur. *The Black Presence in the Bible.* Chicago: Black Light Fellowship, 1990.

Appendix

A BRIEF OUTLINE OF THE BOOK OF GENESIS
1. The Story of Creation (Genesis 1:1–2:3)
2. The Story of Adam and Eve (2:4–4:26)
3. The Story of Adam's Descendants (5:1–6:8)
4. The Story of Noah (6:9–9:29)
5. Table of Nations (10:1-32)
6. The Tower of Babel (11:1-9)
7. The Story of Shem's Descendants (11:10–26)
8. The Story of Terah and Abraham (11:27–25:11)
9. The Story of Ishmael (25:12–18)
10. The Story of Isaac (25:19–35:29)
11. The Story of Esau (36:1–37:1)
12. The Story of Jacob and Joseph (37:2–50:26)

A BRIEF OUTLINE OF THE BOOK OF MATTHEW
1. The Introduction of the King (Matthew 1:1–4:25)
2. The Platform of the King (5:1–7:29)
3. The Credentials of the King (8:1–11:30)
4. The Opposition to the King (12:1–16:12)
5. The Preparation of the King's Disciples (16:13–20:34)
6. The Presentation, Rejection, and Crucifixion of the King (21:1–27:66)
7. The Resurrection and Commission of the King (28:1–20)

A BRIEF OUTLINE OF THE BOOK OF MARK
1. Birth and Preparation of Jesus, the Servant (Mark 1:1–13)
2. Message and Ministry of Jesus, the Servant (1:14–13:37)
   a. Jesus' Ministry in Galilee
   b. Jesus' Ministry beyond Galilee
   c. Jesus' Ministry in Jerusalem
3. Death and Resurrection of Jesus, the Servant (14:1–16:20)

A BRIEF OUTLINE OF THE BOOK OF JOHN
1. Prologue (John 1:1–18)
2. Jesus' Ministry to the World (1–12)
3. Jesus' Ministry to the Disciples (13–17)
4. Jesus' Crucifixion and Resurrection (18–20)
5. Post-Resurrection (21)